MICROWAVE COOKING FOR
Vegetarians

MICROWAVE COOKING FOR Vegetarians

MYRA STREET

CHARTWELL
BOOKS, INC.

MICROWAVE COOKING FOR Vegetarians CONTENTS

A QUINTET BOOK

Published by Chartwell Books
A Division of Book Sales, Inc.
110 Enterprise Avenue
Secaucus, New Jersey 07094

ISBN 1-55521-005-8

This book was designed and produced by
Quintet Publishing Limited
6 Blundell Street
London N7

Art Director: Peter Bridgewater
Editors: Henrietta Wilkinson, Josephine Bacon
Photographers: Trevor Wood and Michael Bull
Home economist: Veronica Bull
Illustrator: Lorraine Harrison
Jacket illustration: Annie Ellis

Typeset in Great Britain by
Central Southern Typesetters, Eastbourne
Manufactured in Hong Kong by
Regent Publishing Services Limited
Printed in Hong Kong by
Leefung-Asco Printers Limited

The author and publisher would like to thank
Toshiba UK Ltd, Corning Microwave Ware and
Thorpak for providing equipment for
recipe-testing and photography.

Contents

Introduction

THE microwave oven must surely be the perfect piece of kitchen equipment for those following a meatless diet. Here, at last, is the ideal way to cook vegetables with minimal liquid and nutrient loss. It is essential to study any diet carefully to provide a balance and particularly if high protein foods like meat and fish are excluded from the meals. Lacto-vegetarian diets which include milk, cheese and eggs are easily balanced, as enough amino-acids are obtained from the proteins in these foods. However, vegetarians who eat no animal proteins need to plan their food intake carefully; their diet tends to be very bulky, since vegetables are a poorer source of protein than animal foods. A vegan diet (one without milk or eggs as well as being meatless) should include peas, beans, soya flour and nuts, all of which are good sources of protein.

Although it is often only one member of a family who is vegetarian, current attitudes on health and fitness are encouraging us all to eat less animal fat. In fact, the whole family will benefit from the variety and change with an increase of vegetable dishes in everyday meals.

Choose the freshest, best-quality vegetables available and when they are out of season, substitute with frozen vegetables.

HOW THE
MICROWAVE OVEN OPERATES

It is best to understand the basic principle behind the microwave oven to obtain good results with the food that you cook in it. Read the manufacturer's instruction book carefully, as there are many different models available. The more expensive ovens have many variable settings; these help to cook dishes which need long, slow cooking in a conventional oven. It is impossible to discuss each microwave oven in detail but it is essential to use your oven every day until it is completely familiar to you. Many people give up if they do not succeed immediately and use it only on the defrost and reheat cycles. However, it is like any new piece of equipment: it does require a little patience and practice to use.

It is useful to know how microwaves work, in order to put them to their best use. A microwave is a short wave similar to those used in radar and radio. It is reflected by metal and absorbed by the water molecules in food. Unlike a conventional oven, which cooks by heat passing through the food from the outside, the microwaves cook the food by vibrating the water molecules in the food. The friction caused cooks the food on the inside at the same time as cooking it on the outside, and so reduces the cooking time.

As the microwaves pass through the cooking utensils the oven itself is not heated. The container only eventually becomes hot from the heat given off by the cooking food. This means that the kitchen remains free from heat, steam and extra dishwashing, as the food can generally be served straight from the microwave oven to the table. The food retains its colour, texture and fresh taste, and also shrinks less than in conventional cooking.

UTENSILS

The following household utensils are unsuitable for cooking in the microwave oven, because microwaves reflect off the metal and will seriously damage the magnetron which makes the oven work.

☛ Dishes or plates with gold or silver rims.
☛ Metal cake tins (pans) or baking trays (cookie sheets).
☛ Metal pots and pans.
☛ Ovenproof glassware with metal attachments.
☛ Food wrapped in foil.
☛ Foil containers of any type.
☛ Avoid plastic and melamine containers except for short defrosting times.
☛ Plastic bags can only withstand short defrosting. Do not use for reheating.

Any other china or kitchen utensils will probably be suitable for use in the microwave oven. If you need to test a dish for microwave use, place it in the oven and stand an ovenproof glass jug filled with ⅓ cup/150 ml/¼ pint cold water in the middle. Switch on at full power for 1 minute, after which the dish should be cold and the water warm. If the dish is even slightly warm it should not be used in the oven. There are many excellent containers made specially for use in microwave ovens if you feel that your ordinary kitchen dishes are unsuitable or the wrong shape.

BROWNING DISHES

These are special glass and ceramic dishes, available in a range of shapes and sizes, which are very useful for lightly browning food. The dish is especially treated to absorb and attract the micro-

waves. The browning dish is put into the oven without food for several minutes to heat. Any food can then be placed on the hot surface and if the dish is quickly returned to the oven the food will brown. To brown both sides, remove and turn during cooking. This is very useful for browning onions and garlic before adding other vegetables as they need cooking in a little butter or oil before they blend in and combine naturally with the other ingredients. Browning dishes must be cleaned carefully to avoid destroying the browning surface; do not use pan scourers but gently soak away any food which has stuck to the dish.

COVERING FOOD IN THE MICROWAVE OVEN

Food is best covered when cooking in the microwave oven to prevent splashing or spattering. This also helps retain the moisture in the food and it cooks more evenly. Many dishes have lids and these are quite suitable, otherwise cling film

(plastic wrap) may be used to cover the dish. If using cling film (plastic wrap), make a slit in the top or turn back one corner: this will stop the covering ballooning as the food is cooked, thus trapping steam which could burn the person removing the film (wrap). Absorbent kitchen towels are useful for covering food like sandwiches, jacket potatoes and poached eggs as the steam penetrates through the paper. Bread and pancakes which are being refreshed can also be wrapped in kitchen towels.

COOKING IN THE MICROWAVE OVEN

The length of time needed to cook food in the microwave oven also depends on the type of oven and the amount of food to be cooked. The best example of this is the baked potato: when one potato will cook in approximately 5–6 minutes, two potatoes of equal size will take 9–10 minutes. Whereas with one potato all the microwaves are being absorbed by the one item of food, double the quantity means the microwaves are spread

more thinly, and this creates a longer cooking time. If the food is very cold when it goes into the oven, it will take longer to cook, as in conventional cooking, so make allowances for a little extra time if it is taken directly out of the refrigerator. Thin, evenly-sliced food will cook more quickly than thick, chunky pieces and this is especially important when cooking vegetables.

TURNING FOOD IN THE
MICROWAVE OVEN

Food cooked in the conventional way is usually turned during cooking, whether under the grill (broiler), or in the oven, and this applies to the microwave as well. Unless the oven instructions state otherwise, food must be rotated from time to time. Some microwave ovens have a turntable which rotates the food automatically as it cooks; but if yours does not, or some dishes are too large for the turntable, turn the plate around by hand, a quarter turn at a time, during cooking.

ARRANGING FOOD IN CONTAINERS
FOR MICROWAVING

Arrange food with the thickest parts towards the outside of the dish. Dishes such as stuffed vegetables should be arranged in a circle leaving the centre clear to ensure more even cooking.

THE RECIPES

I have tried to simplify the instructions in the recipes in this book. Many microwave users complain about the complicated instructions and numerous steps used in some microwave recipes. I have tested them both in a simple, basic microwave oven in which the dishes must be turned manually, and in a more advanced oven with variable power levels and a turntable. The cooking times of the dishes are approximate to within a few minutes, depending on the wattage and size of the oven.

Sauces Etc

RIGHT: *Hollandaise Sauce*

Hollandaise Sauce

INGREDIENTS

SERVES 4
¾ cup/175 g/6 oz butter
2 tbsp wine vinegar or 2 tbsp lemon juice
2 egg yolks
salt and pepper

PREPARATION

☛ Melt the butter on full power for 2 minutes.

☛ Whisk the vinegar or lemon juice in a small bowl with the egg yolks and seasoning.

☛ Pour the melted butter into the bowl, gradually whisking as the butter is added. When half the butter has been incorporated, cook in the microwave oven for 30 seconds; remove and whisk again.

☛ Add remaining butter and cook for 30 seconds. Whisk and, if necessary, cook for a further 30 seconds. Serve immediately.

Mousseline Sauce

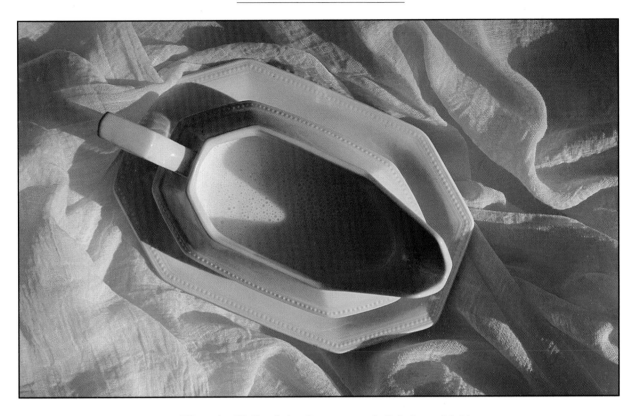

Allow the Hollandaise Sauce to cool slightly and fold in 1 cup/225 ml/8 fl oz whipped double (heavy) cream. Serve with any crisp vegetable for a special occasion.

VARIATION

Add 1 tablespoon chopped gherkins (pickles) or capers for extra flavour.

Tomato Sauce

INGREDIENTS

MAKES 2½ CUPS/600 ML/1 PINT
2 tbsp oil
2 onions, peeled and diced
1 clove garlic, crushed
1 carrot, scraped and grated
2 lb/1 kg/2 lb ripe tomatoes, chopped
1 tsp sugar
1 tbsp chopped basil
1 bay leaf
1 bouquet garni
salt and freshly ground pepper
½ cup/125 ml/4 fl oz white wine or vegetable stock

PREPARATION

☛ Heat the oil for 1 minute in a casserole or bowl. Add the onion and garlic and cook for 2 minutes. Add the carrot and cook on full power for a further 2 minutes.

☛ Stir in all the other ingredients, mix well and cook, covered, for 10 minutes. Allow to stand for 5 minutes. Remove the bay leaf and bouquet garni.

☛ Sieve the sauce to remove the tomato skins. Use as required.

VARIATION

If a rough texture is preferred, skin the tomatoes before cooking. The sauce can then be put through a blender or food processor. If using canned plum tomatoes, add 2 × 14 oz/400 g/14 oz cans.

Toppings for Cooked Vegetables

SERVES 4

½ cup/125 ml/4 fl oz sour cream mixed with 2 tsp chopped chives

¼ cup/50 ml/2 fl oz sour cream mixed with 2–3 tbsp cottage cheese and 2 tsp chopped chives

½ cup/125 ml/4 fl oz yogurt mixed with 1 crushed garlic clove and ½ tsp ground cumin

SAVOURY BUTTERS

A selection of these butters can be made up and stored in the freezer to add flavor to vegetable dishes when needed. Make the butters into a round roll, chill well and then cut into suitable portions for future use. Freeze until hard and then store in individual portions.

INGREDIENTS

LEMON BUTTER

4 tbsp/500 g/2 oz butter

2 tsp lemon juice

salt and freshly ground pepper

1 tbsp chopped parsley

PREPARATION

☛ Soften the butter in the oven on half power for 1 minute.

☛ Cream it with all the other ingredients and then chill for 1 hour in the refrigerator.

☛ Make into a roll and freeze for 30 minutes; cut into portions and pack.

TO SERVE

Use on cooked beans, corn on the cob, cauliflower, brussel sprouts, cabbage, broccoli, asparagus and artichokes.

CORIANDER BUTTER

Substitute 1–2 tbsp chopped coriander for the parsley.

SAGE BUTTER

Substitute 1 tbsp chopped fresh sage leaves for the parsley. This butter is especially good with green beans and tomatoes.

TARRAGON BUTTER

Substitute 2 tsp tarragon sprigs for parsley. A good accompaniment for tomatoes, beans and courgettes (zucchini).

INGREDIENTS

GARLIC BUTTER

4 tbsp/50 g/2 oz butter

1–2 garlic cloves, crushed

1 tbsp chopped parsley or mixed fresh herbs

☛ Make as for Lemon Butter. Serve with mushrooms, courgettes (zucchini), tomatoes, sweet (bell) peppers and aubergines (egg plant).

Pepper Sauce

INGREDIENTS

MAKES 2½ CUPS/600 ML/1 PINT
10 red chilli (chili) peppers, deseeded
¼ cup/50 ml/2 fl oz oil
2 onions, peeled and diced
1–2 cloves garlic, crushed
1 sweet (bell) pepper, deseeded
1 × 14 oz/400 g/14 oz can plum peeled tomatoes
1 tsp salt
2 tsp mustard powder
1¼ cups/300 ml/½ pint wine vinegar
1 bay leaf

PREPARATION

☛ Slice the chilli (chili) peppers thinly: wash your hands afterwards as the peppers can irritate the skin.
☛ Put the oil in a dish or large bowl, then microwave for 1 minute on full power.
☛ Add the onions to the bowl with the garlic and cook for 3 minutes on full power.
☛ Dice the sweet (bell) pepper. Place all the ingredients in the bowl with the onion. Stir well, cover and cook for 10 minutes. Allow to stand.
☛ Cook for a further 10 minutes, allow to stand for 3 minutes.
☛ Strain through a nylon sieve and store in small sterilized bottles or jars. Alternatively, put through a blender or food processor and then push through a nylon sieve. Reheat in the oven for 5 minutes, bottle and seal. Store in the refrigerator.

TO SERVE

Use for flavoring spicy dishes and a few drops gives a different taste to a dressing for salad.

Butterscotch Sauce

INGREDIENTS

SERVES 4
¾ cup/100 g/4 oz soft brown sugar
4 tbsp/50 g/2 oz butter
4 tbsp cream

PREPARATION

☛ Place all the ingredients in a shallow dish. Microwave uncovered on full power for 2 minutes.
☛ Stir well, and then cook on half power for a further 2 minutes or until well mixed.

Béchamel (White) Sauce

INGREDIENTS

SERVES 4
2½ cups/600 ml/1 pt milk
¼ onion, peeled
1 bay leaf
1 bouquet garni
1 slice of carrot
3 tbsp/40 g/1½ oz butter
½ cup/50 g/2 oz plain (all-purpose) flour
salt and pepper

PREPARATION

☛ Put the milk in an ovenproof glass measuring jug with the onion, bay leaf, bouquet garni and carrot. Cook on full power for 3 minutes and allow to stand, covered, for 10 minutes.

☛ Heat the butter in a bowl for 2 minutes, remove from the oven and stir in the flour. Gradually add the strained milk and whisk the mixture until smooth. Season well.

☛ Reheat in the oven at full power for 2 minutes, then remove and whisk. Return to the oven at full power and cook for a further 2 minutes, then whisk again. Cook for another minute, allow to stand for 2 minutes, whisk and leave to stand.

TO SERVE

Use for vegetable dishes with or without first adding herbs and cheese.

Rich Shortcrust Pastry

INGREDIENTS

MAKES 2×7 IN/7 CM FLAN CASES
3 cups/350 g/12 oz plain (all purpose) flour
¾ cup + 2 tbsp/200 g/7 oz block margarine or butter
1 egg yolk
2 tbsp water

PREPARATION

☛ Preheat a conventional oven to 400°F/200°C/Gas Mark 6.

☛ Sift the flour into a bowl and cut the fat into small pieces. Rub it in with the fingertips until the mixture resembles fine breadcrumbs. Make a well in the centre of the mixture and drop in the egg yolk with half the water. Mix with a round-bladed knife (metal spatula), adding the remaining water gradually until the pastry forms a dough which leaves the bowl clean. Knead lightly, wrap in cling film (plastic wrap) and refrigerate for 10 minutes.

☛ Arrange the flan rings on plastic baking (cookie) sheets or use flan dishes.

☛ Roll out half the pastry to fit the ring or dish with 2 in/5 cm to spare. Lift the pastry carefully on the rolling pin and ease into the ring. Press gently into the shape of the ring without stretching. Trim the top with the rolling pin or a sharp knife if using a china dish.

☛ Prick the bottom with a fork and line with a round of greaseproof (non-stick baking) paper. Cover with baking beans and cook in the oven for 15 minutes. Remove the baking beans and cook for a further 10 minutes.

Note It is possible to cook the pastry in a plain china flan dish in the microwave oven but the resulting pastry is less attractive.

To do this, cover the edges of the flan with a thin strip of foil to prevent drying out. Cover the flan with kitchen towels and cook for 4 minutes on full power. Remove the foil and paper and cook for a further 2 minutes.

Spring Dishes

RIGHT: *Piperade*

Piperade

This version of the Basque speciality without ham is easy and delicious cooked in the microwave oven.

INGREDIENTS

SERVES 4
¼ cup/50 ml/2 fl oz vegetable oil
1 garlic clove
1 small onion, peeled and diced
2 spring onions (scallions), sliced
1 sweet red (bell) pepper, deseeded
1 green (bell) pepper, deseeded
1 bouquet garni
1 bay leaf
2 large tomatoes, skinned
salt and freshly ground black pepper
8 eggs
2 tbsp/25 g/1 oz butter, cut into small pieces

PREPARATION

☛ Heat the vegetable oil in a browning dish. Slightly crush the garlic clove but leave it whole and add it to the dish. Cook for 30 seconds at full power in the oil.
☛ Add the onions and spring onions (scallions) to the garlic and cook on half power for 6 minutes.
☛ Prepare the peppers by pouring boiling water over them in a bowl and leaving them to stand for 2 minutes. If preferred, prepare them the traditional way by charring under a hot grill (broiler) and then removing the flesh from the skin. Chop the peppers very finely by hand or in a food processor, taking care not to liquidize them completely. Add them to the onion and cook on full power for a further 5 minutes with the bouquet garni and bay leaf.
☛ Remove the seeds from the tomatoes, chop finely and add to the vegetable mixture. Season well and cook on full for a further 5 minutes.
☛ Beat the eggs in a bowl with ¼ cup/50 ml/2 fl oz water. Add the butter.
☛ Remove the bouquet garni, bay leaf and garlic from the tomato mixture and stir in the eggs. Cook on full power for 4 minutes, remove and mix well.
☛ Return to the microwave oven, cook for a further 4 minutes. Remove and stir again. If the mixture is too liquid, cook for a further 2 minutes and test after stirring.

Note Remember that the mixture thickens very quickly at this stage and the delicious, creamy eggs can toughen if microwaved for a few seconds too long.

TO SERVE

Sprinkle with chopped spring onions (scallions) and triangles of toast.
This dish can also be used to fill savoury pastry shells and is particularly good as a starter.

Eggs Provençale

INGREDIENTS

SERVES 4

8 tomatoes, skinned and sliced

1 tbsp vegetable oil

1 garlic clove, crushed

1 sprig of parsley

1 sprig of thyme

1 bay leaf

salt and freshly ground pepper

¼ tsp sugar

4 eggs

2 tsp chopped parsley

PREPARATION

☛ Place all the ingredients except the eggs and parsley in a microwave bowl. Cook on full power for 5 minutes, stir and cook for a further 5 minutes.

☛ Remove the tomato sauce from the microwave oven, take out the sprigs of herbs and the bay leaf. Sieve or blend the sauce, taste and correct seasoning.

☛ Butter 4 ramekin individual dishes, and divide the tomato mixture between them.

☛ Break the eggs one at a time into a cup and pour into the centre of each dish. Sterilize a skewer or large needle by dipping it in boiling water and use it to prick the yolks.

☛ Season the eggs and place the dishes in the microwave oven. Cook on full power for 1 minute, then reduce to half power and cook for a further 5 minutes. Allow to stand for 1–2 minutes before serving.

TO SERVE

Sprinkle with chopped parsley and serve with fingers of toast.

Eggs Florentine

INGREDIENTS

SERVES 4

half quantity creamed spinach recipe

4 eggs

salt and freshly ground pepper

4 tbsp cream

PREPARATION

☛ Prepare the creamed spinach. Butter four ramekin (individual china) dishes and divide the spinach between them.

☛ Make a well in the centre of each dish with the back of a spoon. Break the eggs into a cup one at a time and slide each into a bed of spinach. Prick the yolks with a sterilised needle, season with salt and pepper and carefully pour the cream over the top.

☛ Stand the dishes in a deep glass dish. Pour some boiling water around them. Cook in the microwave oven for 4 minutes at full power. Check to see if the eggs are cooked; if not, cook for a further 1 minute or to taste.

Note If cooking the dishes individually, check after 1½ minutes.

TO SERVE

Sprinkle with chopped parsley and triangles of toast.

Globe Artichokes

INGREDIENTS

SERVES 4

4 globe artichokes

1 lemon, juice squeezed or 2 tbsp vinegar

PREPARATION

☛ Choose firm, fresh-looking artichokes: if the leaves are open, it is advisable to soak them in a basin of water with some added vinegar to remove any earth and insects. Trim off the stalks. Some people like to snip the top from the leaves to give the leaves a square cut appearance.

☛ Both these methods of cooking artichokes in the microwave are successful.

a) Place the artichokes in a large casserole or bowl with 2½ cups/600 ml/1 pt water, the juice of 1 lemon or 2 tbsp of vinegar. Cook on full power for 10 minutes. Change round the positions and test by pulling off a leaf from the outside. Unless the artichokes are very fresh you will probably find that they will need a further 10 minutes at full power but test again after 5 minutes. When a leaf pulls away easily you know that the artichokes are ready for eating. Drain upside down on a wire rack before serving.

b) Arrange the artichokes on a piece of cling film (plastic wrap), pour a little water and lemon juice into the leaves, wrap loosely and make a slit in the top of the cling film (plastic wrap). Cook on full power for 6 minutes for 1 artichoke or 25 minutes for 4. Allow to stand for 2–3 minutes and then drain upside down on a wire rack.

TO SERVE

Serve hot with Hollandaise Sauce (see page 12) or melted butter. Serve cold with mayonnaise or vinaigrette dressing.

Stuffed Artichokes

INGREDIENTS

SERVES 4

4 globe artichokes

1 lemon, rind and juice

½ cup/25 g/1 oz soft breadcrumbs

1 cup/100 g/4 oz mushrooms

salt and freshly ground pepper

1 spring onion (scallion)

¼ cup/50 ml/2 fl oz cream

4 slices Gruyère cheese

2 tbsp/25 g/1 oz butter

PREPARATION

☛ Prepare the artichokes: cut off the stalks and remove the two rows of outer leaves with a sharp knife or scissors. The shaped artichokes should then stand on a plate evenly. Cut across the top of each artichoke about 1 in/2½ cm from the top giving a flat top.

☛ Put the prepared artichokes in a covered casserole dish with water and half the lemon juice. Cook on full power for 20 minutes. Remove and drain upside down on a wire rack.

☛ Push down with three fingers into the middle section of the leaves and pull these out, leaving the choke visible. Remove it with a teaspoon, making sure that you do not scrape away the heart.

☛ Mix the breadcrumbs in a bowl with the finely grated lemon rind. Chop the mushrooms and tip into the breadcrumbs, season well with salt and pepper. Add the chopped spring onion (scallion) and mix in the cream.

☛ Stuff the artichoke hearts with the mixture and lay a slice of cheese on top of the stuffing.

☛ Lay the artichokes on a flat plate, cover with cling film (plastic wrap) and cook on full power for 5 minutes. Allow to stand for 2 minutes.

☛ Melt the butter and mix it with the remaining lemon juice.

TO SERVE

Pour a little butter and lemon juice over each artichoke.

Dauphinois Potatoes

INGREDIENTS

SERVES 4

2 lb/1 kg/2 lb small new potatoes

1¼ cups/300 ml/½ pint milk

1 bay leaf

2 sprigs of parsley

1 slice of onion

salt and pepper

2 tbsp/25 g/1 oz butter

1 cup/225 ml/8 fl oz double (heavy) cream

1 garlic clove, crushed

PREPARATION

☛ Prick the new potatoes with a fork, arrange in a dish with 1 cup/225 ml/8 fl oz salted water. Cook in the microwave oven at full power for 10 minutes. Allow to stand for 3 minutes.

☛ Drain and peel the potatoes (or leave the skins on if you prefer) and slice them thinly.

☛ Heat the milk in a jug with the bay leaf, parsley, onion slice and salt and pepper.

☛ Butter a browning dish and rub over with the garlic cloves. Arrange the sliced potatoes in rings, strain over the hot milk and then cook, uncovered, at full power for 10 minutes.

☛ Remove, season the potatoes well and pour over the cream. Microwave on full power for 3 minutes, and then allow to stand for 3 minutes.

TO SERVE

Lightly brown under a hot grill (broiler).

Hot Oatmeal Potatoes

INGREDIENTS

SERVES 4

2 lb/1 kg/2 lb new potatoes, scrubbed

¼ cup/50 g/2 oz butter

6 spring onions (scallions)

½ cup/75 g/3 oz porridge oats
(quick-cooking oatmeal flakes)

¼ cup/50 ml/2 fl oz cream (optional)

1 tbsp chopped parsley

PREPARATION

☛ Prick the new potatoes several times with a fork. Place in a deep dish with 1 cup/225 ml/8 fl oz salted water. Cover with a lid or cling film (plastic wrap) and microwave on full power for 10 minutes. Allow to stand for 3 minutes.

☛ Test the potatoes: if they are not quite cooked, give the dish a quarter turn and cook for a further 3 minutes. Drain, and then cut the potatoes into even slices.

☛ Melt the butter in a dish. Add four chopped spring onions (scallions), stir well, and mix in the sliced potatoes and the oatmeal. Cook on full power for 5 minutes. Add ¼ cup/50 ml/2 fl oz cream to the potatoes if liked.

TO SERVE

Sprinkle with the remaining two chopped spring onions (scallions) and the parsley.

Cannelloni with Spinach and Ricotta

INGREDIENTS

SERVES 4

1½ cups/350 g/12 oz cooked chopped or frozen spinach

2 cups/225 g/8 oz ricotta cheese

¼ tsp grated nutmeg

salt and pepper

12 precooked cannelloni tubes

2 cups/400 g/16 fl oz canned sieved tomatoes

1 tsp chopped basil

2 tbsp/25 g/1 oz butter

1 onion, peeled and diced

¼ tsp oregano

2½ cups/600 ml/1 pt Béchamel Sauce (page 19)

½ cup/50 g/2 oz grated cheese

1 tbsp chopped parsley

PREPARATION

☛ Mix the cooked or defrosted spinach with the ricotta cheese, nutmeg and seasoning.
☛ Spoon or pipe into the cannelloni tubes.
☛ Season the tomatoes with salt, pepper and basil. Place a layer of them in the bottom of a glass or china dish.
☛ Heat the butter in another small dish for 1 minute. Add the onion and cook on full power for 3 minutes. Stir in the oregano. Pour this over the tomato mixture. Arrange the cannelloni tubes on the tomato and onion.
☛ Cover with the Béchamel Sauce and cook for 5 minutes.
☛ Quickly brown under a hot grill (broiler).

TO SERVE

Mix the remaining cheese with the parsley, and sprinkle over the dish.

Aubergines (Eggplant) Italian Style

INGREDIENTS

SERVES 4

2 large aubergines (eggplants), washed
½ cup/125 ml/4 fl oz oil
1 onion, peeled and diced
2 garlic cloves, crushed
14 oz/400 g/14 oz can tomatoes, drained
1 tsp chopped basil
1 bouquet garni
1 bay leaf
salt and pepper
¼ lb/100 g/4 oz Mozzarella cheese

PREPARATION

☛ Halve the aubergines (eggplant) lengthwise, sprinkle the surface with salt and lemon juice and stand upside down on a plate for 20 minutes.

☛ Heat ¼ cup/50 ml/2 fl oz oil in a bowl for 1 minute. Add the onion and garlic, cook on full power for 2 minutes. Stir and cook for a further 1 minute or until the onions are transparent.

☛ Add the chopped tomatoes with the basil, bouquet garni, bay leaf, salt and pepper. Cook on full power covered with cling film (plastic wrap) with a slit on top for 5 minutes, and allow to stand for 2 minutes.

☛ Drain the aubergines (eggplant) and pat dry with paper towels. Prick the skin side several times with a fork, brush with oil all over. Arrange on an oiled dish and cook, covered, for 10 minutes on full power. Allow to stand for 2 minutes. Cut out the flesh of the cooked aubergines (eggplant) and chop into small dice.

☛ Add the aubergine (eggplant) flesh to the tomato mixture. Season the inside of the aubergines (eggplant) and paint with oil. Fill with tomato mixture, return to the microwave and cook on full power for 8 minutes. Remove.

☛ Top each aubergine (eggplant) half with slices of Mozzarella cheese, paint with oil and return for 2 minutes on full until the cheese starts to melt.

TO SERVE

If liked, brown under a hot grill (broiler) to finish.

Vegetable Loaf

INGREDIENTS

SERVES 6

½ lb/225 g/8 oz broccoli spears

2 carrots, grated

3 celery stalks, tops discarded

2 tbsp/25 g/1 oz butter

2 tbsp/25 g/1 oz flour

3 eggs

salt and pepper

¼ tsp paprika

¼ tsp mustard powder

½ cup/100 g/4 oz cottage cheese

1 cup/100 g/4 oz grated Cheddar cheese

2 tomatoes, skinned

2 spring onions (scallions), washed and trimmed

PREPARATION

☛ Arrange the broccoli spears in a ring on a shallow dish with heads to the centre of the dish. Sprinkle with 2–3 tbsp water, cover and cook for 8 minutes at full power.

☛ Remove the dish, arrange the grated carrot in heaps and the celery in 1 in/2½ cm pieces between the stalks. Cover and cook for 5 minutes at full power, drain.

☛ Melt the butter for 1 minute in a bowl at full power, then stir in the flour. Gradually beat in the eggs and season them well with salt, pepper, paprika and mustard. Beat in the cottage cheese and then the grated cheese.

☛ Mix the cheese mixture with broccoli, celery and carrot. Cook on full power for 3 minutes, stir well.

☛ Butter a glass loaf pan or a rectangular china terrine dish. Cover the bottom of the dish with the sliced tomatoes and chopped spring onions (scallions), then arrange half the cooked mixture in the dish. Pour on the remaining mixture, cover and cook on full for 3 minutes. Turn power to half, or defrost, cook for a further 6 . Allow to stand for 3 minutes.

☛ Test to make sure the mixture is cooked. Unmould (unmold) the dish on to a heated plate and test the bottom with a fork.

Cut into slices and serve with Tomato Sauce (see page 15) and new potatoes.

Broccoli/Cauliflower Cheese

INGREDIENTS

SERVES 4

1 lb/450 g/1 lb fresh broccoli, washed or
¾ lb/350 g/12 oz frozen pack

1 cauliflower, washed

2 potatoes, peeled

2½ cups/600 ml/1 pint Béchamel (White) Sauce
(see page 19)

2 tbsp/25 g/1 oz butter

salt and freshly ground pepper

¼ cup/50 ml/2 fl oz milk

4 slices cheese

1 tbsp crisp breadcrumbs

PREPARATION

☛ Arrange the broccoli in a round dish with the spears facing in to the centre and stalks out. Add 4 tsp salted water and cook on full power for 5 minutes, covered.

☛ If using frozen, thaw first and only cook for 3 minutes at this stage.

☛ Arrange the cauliflower florets in the same dish in a ring when the broccoli is finished and removed to a plate. Cook on full power for 5 minutes and then allow to stand for 3 minutes.

☛ While the vegetables are cooking, slice the potatoes thinly, use the food processor if you have one. Make up the Béchamel Sauce.

☛ Arrange the potatoes on the bottom of a buttered deep dish. Add salt and pepper to the milk, pour over the potatoes, partially cover with a lid or with cling film (plastic wrap). Microwave on full power for 5 minutes, allow longer if the potato slices are chunky. Stand for 3 minutes.

☛ Arrange the broccoli spears facing in to the centre in a ring, alternating with the cauliflower.

☛ Pour over the well-seasoned Béchamel Sauce and microwave for 10 minutes on full power. Sprinkle with freshly ground pepper and cover with the slices of cheese. Microwave on full for 2 minutes or until the cheese has melted. Sprinkle with the breadcrumbs and brown under the grill (broiler), if liked. Allow to stand for 2 minutes and then serve while the cheese is still soft.

Soufflé Omelette (Omelet)

INGREDIENTS

SERVES 2
4 eggs, separated
¼ cup/50 ml/2 fl oz water
salt and pepper
2 tbsp/25 g/1 oz butter

If the omelette (omelet) is to be filled, prepare the fillings before whisking the eggs.

PREPARATION

☛ Mix the egg yolks in a bowl with the water and seasoning.
☛ Whisk the egg whites until light and fluffy to make mixing easier.
☛ Take a metal spoon and fold the egg whites gradually into the yolks.
☛ Meanwhile, place the butter in a browning dish in the microwave oven and heat for 1 minute on full power. Pour in the egg mixture and cook on high for 30 seconds. Open the door and lift up the mixture gently, allowing any excess to run under the omelette (omelet). Cook on half power for 3 minutes or until set. Add the filling and serve.

TO SERVE

Turn over or quickly brown under a hot grill (broiler) for a golden finish.

ONION AND PEPPER

Dice a small onion and a small, deseeded (bell) pepper. Cook in the microwave at full power for 3 minutes. Sprinkle with ¼ cup/25 g/1 oz grated cheese if liked.

MUSHROOM

Wash and slice 1 cup/100 g/4 oz mushrooms. Heat 1 tbsp/25 g/1 oz butter in a dish for 30 seconds at full power. Add the mushrooms and cook covered with cling film (plastic wrap) for 3 minutes. Mix with 1 tbsp chopped parsley. Fill the omelette (omelet) and turn over.

CORN AND PEPPER

Heat a knob of butter in the microwave oven at full power for 30 seconds. Add half a diced (bell) pepper and cook for 2 minutes. Mix in 4 tbsp canned sweet corn and heat for 45 seconds to 1 minute.

TOMATO AND HERB

Skin 2 large tomatoes and cut into slices. Sprinkle with 2 chopped spring onions (scallions) and a few chopped basil leaves. Add to the omelette (omelet), return to the microwave for 30 seconds, fold over and serve.

SAUCE FILLING

A few tablespoons of Béchamel (White) or Tomato Sauce (see pages 19 and 15) can be added to any of the above vegetable fillings for a more substantial meal.

Lemon Curd

INGREDIENTS

MAKES 1 ½ LB / 750 G / 1 ½ LB

2 cups/450 g/1 lb sugar

4 lemons, rind grated, juice squeezed

¾ cup/175 g/6 oz butter

6 eggs, beaten

PREPARATION

☛ Put the sugar in a glass bowl.
☛ Mix the butter into the sugar and cook on full power for 1 minute.
☛ Add the rind and juice of the lemons to the butter and sugar and mix well. Strain in the beaten eggs, whisking the mixture well.
☛ Cook on full power for 2 minutes, remove and stir well. Return to the oven and cook for a further 6 minutes, removing every 2 minutes to stir.
☛ Test the mixture to see that it is smooth and thick. Pot in sterilized jars and store in a cool place.

TO SERVE

Lemon curd has a limited shelf life and is best eaten within two weeks unless kept in the refrigerator.

VARIATION

Use egg yolks to make the curd if you have an excess, using two whole eggs and four egg yolks.

Three Fruits Marmalade

INGREDIENTS

MAKES 6×1 LB/450 G/1 LB JARS

1 lb/450 g/1 lb oranges

1 grapefruit

2 lemons

7½ cups/1.7 l/3 pt water

3 lb/1.4 kg/3 lb sugar

PREPARATION

Note: This easy, cleaner way of making delicious marmalade only needs stirring occasionally. However, it is essential that the sugar is dissolved by stirring before boiling for a second time.

☛ Cook the fruit in two batches in the microwave oven on full power for 3 minutes each.

☛ Cut the fruit in half and squeeze out the juice. Slice the skins with a sharp knife or the small slicing blade for a food processor. Put the pips (seeds) in a piece of muslin or fine rinsed cloth and tie the top of the bag securely.

☛ Use a large bowl or 4 qt/4 L/7 pt casserole. Place the pips (seeds), sliced skin and water in it, turn to full power and heat the water for 45 minutes.

☛ Stir in the sugar until it is dissolved. If necessary, give it a three minute burst of full power, remove and stir to dissolve the sugar. Use oven gloves, as the bowl of fruit will be hot and needs handling carefully.

☛ When the sugar has dissolved, replace the bowl and microwave at full power for 1 hour. Stir after 10 minutes, skim any foam from the surface and continue cooking.

☛ Test for setting on a cold plate: if a spoonful of marmalade wrinkles after 1 minute, it has reached setting point and is ready.

☛ Ladle into warm sterilized jars, seal and label.

VARIATION

Orange marmalade: Use 2 lb/1 kg/2 lb Seville (bitter) oranges and 1 lemon. Make as above.

Summer Dishes

RIGHT: *Aubergine (Eggplant) Savoury Slices*

Aubergine (Eggplant) Savoury Slices

INGREDIENTS

SERVES 4

4 aubergines (eggplants)

salt and pepper

1 lemon, juice

½ cup/125 ml/4 fl oz vegetable oil

1 garlic clove, chopped (minced)

¾ lb/350 g/12 oz Mozzarella or Lancashire cheese

8 tomatoes, skinned

½ cup/6 tbsp chopped parsley or basil

PREPARATION

☛ Cut the aubergines (eggplants) into 16 even slices. Arrange the slices on a tray or covered with kitchen towels and sprinkle with salt and lemon juice. Allow to stand for 20 minutes. Drain and pat dry with fresh paper.

☛ Heat the oil with the chopped (minced) garlic clove in a flat dish for 1 minute on full power. Remove the garlic and cook the first batch of aubergine (eggplant) slices for 3 minutes on full. Turn over and cook for another 2 minutes. Remove from the oil, drain, and continue until all the slices are cooked.

☛ Place four slices on a serving dish and sprinkle with salt and pepper. Cover with slices of cheese and tomato and sprinkle with herbs. Top with another slice of aubergine (eggplant) and finish with slices of cheese and tomato.

☛ Cook four aubergine (eggplant) savouries in a serving dish for 4 minutes or until the cheese is melted. Keep warm while you cook the remaining four.

TO SERVE

Sprinkle with chopped herbs.

Borscht

This is a delicious summer soup which can be prepared in minutes with a food processor. If grating the vegetables by hand, it takes a little longer.

INGREDIENTS

SERVES 4
4 medium/450 g/1 lb beetroot (beets), washed
3 spring onions (scallions)
2 carrots
2 potatoes, peeled
2 courgettes (zucchini)
1 bouquet garni
1 bay leaf
salt and pepper
1 qt/1 l/1¾ pt vegetable stock
½ cup/125 ml/4 fl oz yogurt
1 lemon
1 tbsp chopped chives

PREPARATION

☛ Trim the beetroot (beets) and remove any damaged skin. Arranged in a circle in a casserole, cover with water and cook on full power for 10 minutes. Allow to stand for 2 minutes. Cool.
☛ Chop the spring onions (scallions) and grate the carrots and potatoes coarsely in a food processor. Grate the cooked beetroot (beets).
☛ Put all the vegetables in a large bowl or casserole with the bouquet garni, bay leaf and seasoning. Add the stock, cover and cook at full power for 15 minutes.
☛ Slice the courgettes (zucchini) into thin strips, add to the soup and cook for a further 10 minutes. Test the vegetables and cook for a longer time if they are still too raw.

Serve either hot or cold. Garnish with yogurt flavoured with lemon juice and chopped chives.

Note This soup was tested with young, garden-fresh vegetables. If using shop-bought vegetables, the cooking time may take a further 10 minutes. This soup freezes well but is best served hot, after freezing. Sour cream can be used in place of yogurt.

Mixed Vegetable Lasagne

INGREDIENTS

SERVES 4

1 aubergine (eggplant)

2 courgettes (zucchini)

½ tsp salt

1 lemon, juice

2 tbsp/25 g/1 oz butter

1 garlic clove, crushed

2½ cups/600 ml/1 pt Tomato Sauce (see page 15)

2½ cups/600 ml/1 pt Béchamel Sauce (see page 19)

1 cup/100 g/4 oz mushroom caps

pepper

3 tbsp vegetable oil

16 sheets of lasagne, pre-cooked

¼ cup/25 g/1 oz grated Parmesan cheese

¼ cup/25 g/1 oz fresh breadcrumbs

PREPARATION

☛ Slice the aubergine (eggplant) and courgettes (zucchini) and sprinkle with salt and lemon juice. Allow to stand for 20 minutes.

☛ Rub a large square dish with a little butter mixed with the garlic.

☛ Make up the Tomato and Béchamel Sauces.

☛ Cut the mushrooms into slices including the trimmed stalks.

☛ Drain the aubergines (eggplants) and courgettes (zucchini) and pat dry with absorbent kitchen towels. Heat the oil in a flat dish and cook the aubergines (eggplants) and courgettes (zucchini) in batches for 3 minutes, each batch arranged flat on the dish.

☛ Place a little of the Tomato and Béchamel Sauces on the serving dish for the lasagne. Cover with the sheets of lasagne. Spread with a little Tomato Sauce and a layer of aubergine (eggplant), courgettes (zucchini) and mushrooms, finishing with Béchamel Sauce.

☛ Season well and continue layering. Arrange all the vegetables between the first 2 layers of pasta.

☛ Top with the remaining Tomato and Béchamel sauce. Microwave on full power for 10 minutes. Allow to stand for 5 minutes and then cook for a further 5 minutes on full.

☛ Sprinkle with mixed fresh breadcrumbs and Parmesan cheese. Cook for a further 5 minutes and then brown under the grill (broiler) if required. This makes an ideal main course with green salad.

Lettuce Soup

INGREDIENTS

SERVES 4
2 tbsp/25 g/1 oz butter
1 onion, peeled
1 potato, peeled
2½ cups/600 ml/1 pt vegetable stock (broth)
2 lettuces
1 tsp fresh chervil or chives
salt and pepper
½ cup/125 ml/4 fl oz single cream (half-and-half)
1 spring onion (scallion)

PREPARATION

☛ Melt the butter in a large casserole on full power for 1 minute. Slice the onion and potato finely.
☛ Stir the onion and potato into the butter and cook on full power for 5 minutes; allow to stand for 2 minutes.
☛ Add the vegetable stock and cook for a further 5 minutes. Remove from the microwave and stir in the lettuce, chervil or chives and seasoning. Cook on full power for a further 10 minutes. Allow to stand until slightly cool.
☛ Put the mixture through a coarse sieve, food mill or blender. Reheat as required.

TO SERVE

Add swirls of single (half-and-half) cream before serving and garnish with finely chopped spring onion (scallions). Serve hot or cold.

Asparagus

INGREDIENTS

SERVES 4

1½ lb/700 g/1½ lb asparagus

½ tsp lemon juice

PREPARATION

☛ Trim the asparagus stalks to roughly equal lengths, trimming away the fibrous ends.

☛ Arrange the spears in a dish with sides, tips to the centre and stalks to the edges.

☛ Add enough water to come half-way up the asparagus. Add the lemon juice and cook for 4 minutes at full power. Leave to stand for 2 minutes.

☛ To test for tenderness, prick with a fork. If it needs longer, cook for a further 1 minute at a time until done. Thick spears will probably need 8–10 minutes.

☛ Drain, retaining the water for soup .

TO SERVE

To serve hot, pour melted butter, Hollandaise Sauce (see page 12) or sour cream with lemon juice over the asparagus.

Serve cold with vinaigrette dressing, mayonnaise, Mousseline Sauce (see page 13) or lemon juice and yogurt dressing.

Leek and Tomato Flan

INGREDIENTS

SERVES 4

---

2 leeks

---

1 shortcrust pastry flan case (see page 19)

---

4 tomatoes, skinned

---

2 eggs

¼ cup/50 ml/2 fl oz cream

---

salt and pepper

PREPARATION

☛ Slice the leeks into rings, retaining some of the green part. Put them into a shallow dish with 2 tbsp water. Cover and cook on full power for 3 minutes. Allow to stand for 2 minutes.

☛ Drain the leeks and arrange them in the bottom of the flan case. Slice the tomatoes into rings and arrange on top of the leeks.

☛ Beat the eggs in a bowl with the cream and season well with salt and pepper. Pour this over the leek and tomato mixture, gently easing the vegetables with a fork to allow the egg mixture to flow through the flan.

☛ Microwave on full power for 2 minutes. Cook on half power for a further 6 minutes. Allow to stand for 2 minutes.

TO SERVE

Use hot or cold with salad or a baked vegetable dish.

VARIATIONS

ONION AND (BELL) PEPPER FLAN

Cut 2 medium-sized onions into rings. Cook in 2 tbsp/25 g/1 oz butter on full power for 2 minutes. Deseed and dice a sweet (bell) pepper and add it to the onion and cook for 2 minutes. Arrange in the flan case and continue as above.

ASPARAGUS FLAN

Arrange 1 can drained asparagus on the flan case, reserving a few spears for garnish. Add ½ cup/50 g/ 2 oz grated cheese to the egg mixture. Cook for 3 minutes on full power, remove and decorate with asparagus spears. Cook for 2 minutes.

SWEET CORN AND (BELL) PEPPER FLAN

Defrost 225 g/8 oz frozen sweet corn; drain well. Add 2 tbsp/25 g/1 oz butter and 1 deseeded diced (bell) pepper and cook on full power for 2 minutes. Mix with the egg and cream mixture, pour into the flan and cook as for Leek and Tomato Flan.

MUSHROOM FLAN

Cook 1 cup/100 g/4 oz sliced mushrooms in 2 tbsp/ 25 g/1 oz butter on full power for 2 minutes. Mix with the egg and cream mixture and cook as for Leek and Tomato Flan.

VEGETABLE FLAN

Make up 1½ cups/300 ml/½ pt Cheese Sauce (see page 19). Mix with any favourite vegetable or a mixture of vegetables and cook for 3 minutes on full power. For a golden topping, sprinkle with a mixture of 1 tbsp breadcrumbs mixed with 1 tbsp grated Parmesan cheese. Brown quickly under a hot grill (broiler).

SUITABLE VEGETABLES

☛ ½ lb/250 g/8 oz broccoli
☛ ½ lb/250 g/8 oz sweet corn and peas
☛ ½ lb/250 g/8 oz sliced mushrooms and sweet peppers

Strawberry Jam

INGREDIENTS

MAKES 4×1 LB/450 G/1 LB JARS

5½ cups/1 kg/2 lb strawberries, hulled

1 lemon, juice

4 cups/1 kg/2 lb sugar

PREPARATION

☛ Put the fruit in a large bowl or casserole with the lemon juice and cook for 5 minutes on full power. Mash the strawberries slightly with a wooden spoon.
☛ Add the sugar and stir well. Cook for 3 minutes on full power and stir again. Cook on full for a further 3 minutes and stir to check the sugar is dissolved. If necessary, cook for a further 2 minutes on full power.
☛ Cook for another 6 minutes on full power, stir round thoroughly and cook for a further 6 minutes on full power.
☛ Test on a cold plate; the jam should wrinkle after 1 minute. If not, cook for another 2 minutes on full power.
☛ Pour or ladle into sterilized jars, seal and label.

VARIATION

RASPBERRY JAM

Cook as for strawberry jam but once the sugar has dissolved, cook for a further 15 minutes on full power.

Salad Provençale

INGREDIENTS

SERVES 4

4 cups/450 g/1 lb whole green beans

4 spring onions (scallions)

1 tsp thyme

1 green (bell) pepper, deseeded

1 red (bell) pepper, deseeded

4 tomatoes, skinned

4 hard-boiled (hard-cooked) eggs

½ cup/125 ml/4 fl oz olive oil

1 tsp French mustard

3 tbsp/4 tbsp wine vinegar

1 garlic clove

20 black olives

1 lettuce

PREPARATION

☛ Trim the beans, arrange in a dish with 2 tbsp water, cover and cook on full power for 10 minutes.
☛ Chop all but two of the spring onions (scallions) finely. Add the chopped spring onions (scallions) with the thyme to the beans after 5 minutes of cooking. Mix well and cook for another 5 minutes. Drain and allow to cool.
☛ Slice the peppers into strips and arrange them in a shallow dish. Cover with 3 tbsp water and cook for 5 minutes on full power. Drain and allow to cool.
☛ Cut each tomato into eight wedges and each egg into six wedges lengthwise.
☛ To make the dressing, mix the oil, mustard, vinegar, salt and pepper in a screw-top jar and shake well.
☛ Take a large salad bowl and rub it with a cut clove of garlic. Line with lettuce leaves, and put the beans mixed with half the dressing in the bottom of the bowl. Arrange the peppers, tomatoes and eggs on top with the black olives. Chop the reserved spring onions (scallions) and sprinkle them over the dish. Add rest of the dressing just before serving. Serve with slices of wholemeal or French bread.

Sweet Pepper Hors D'Oeuvre

INGREDIENTS

SERVES 4

4 red, green or yellow (bell) peppers, deseeded

½ cup/125 ml/4 fl oz vegetable oil

1 garlic clove, peeled

2 lemons

salt and freshly ground pepper

1 tsp marjoram

PREPARATION

☛ Slice the peppers into thin strips.

☛ Place the peppers in a flat dish. Avoid piling the strips on top of each other. Add ¼ cup/50 ml/2 fl oz water, cook, covered, on full power for 2 minutes, and then drain.

☛ Place the oil and crushed garlic in a microwave serving dish. Cook on full power for 2 minutes. Add the pepper strips and cook, covered, for 5 minutes on full power.

☛ Allow to cool, sprinkle with lemon juice and seasoning.

TO SERVE

Chill and serve as a starter or with salad.

Mimosa Beans

INGREDIENTS

SERVES 4

1 lb/450 g/1 lb green beans, trimmed and sliced

½ tsp salt

4 hard-boiled (hard-cooked) eggs

2 tbsp/25 g/1 oz butter

1 tsp chopped sage

1 tbsp chopped parsley

freshly ground pepper

1 cup/225 ml/8 fl oz natural (plain) yogurt

PREPARATION

☛ Place the beans in a large casserole. Mix the salt with 2 tbsp water and pour round the beans. Cook, covered, at full power for 5 minutes. Stir and then cook for a further 5 minutes. Allow to stand for 2 minutes and test to see if the beans are done.

☛ While the beans are cooking, cut two eggs into rings, and sieve, separately, the yolks and whites of the other two. Mix the butter with the herbs and some pepper.

☛ Add the butter to the beans and stir well, cook on full power for 2 minutes.

☛ Pour the yogurt over the hot beans and decorate with rings of egg white and yellow egg yolk with rings of sliced egg in the middle. Heat in the microwave for 30 seconds covered.

TO SERVE

This dish is especially good with fresh young beans. Serve hot. Cold leftovers make an excellent salad.

Quick Lunch Pizzas

INGREDIENTS

SERVES 4

4 thick slices wholemeal (wholewheat) bread

1 tbsp vegetable oil

2 large tomatoes, sliced

8 slices yellow cheese

1 tsp freshly ground black pepper

1 tsp chopped basil

16 pitted olives

1 tbsp capers

PREPARATION

☛ Toast one side of the bread under the grill.
☛ Brush the untoasted side of the bread lightly with oil and arrange one layer of tomatoes on top. Sprinkle with freshly ground pepper and basil.
☛ Place the sliced cheese on top, covering the centre but allowing some space for it to melt to the edge of the bread. Cover with remaining slices of tomato.
☛ Decorate with olives and capers and brush with oil. Arrange on a plate and microwave at full power for 3 minutes. Check to see if the cheese has melted and spread and if not, return for a further 1 minute. The cooking time will depend on the type and thickness of the cheese used.

These are ideal winter snacks and an excellent way of using up left over cheese. Toppings can be varied to suit individual tastes:
☛ strips of pepper
☛ green olives
☛ oregano or mixed herbs
☛ sliced mushrooms
☛ sliced aubergines (eggplants)

Green Beans and Red (Bell) Peppers

INGREDIENTS

SERVES 4
4 cups/450 g/1 lb green beans, trimmed and sliced
3 tbsp/2 tbsp vegetable oil
1 onion, peeled and finely chopped
1 red (bell) pepper, deseeded and diced
1 garlic clove, crushed
4 tomatoes, skinned, chopped
2 tsp chopped sage or basil

PREPARATION

☛ Place the beans in a deep dish with ¼ cup/50 ml/ 2 fl oz water, cover and cook for 4 minutes. Allow to stand for 2 minutes.

☛ Put the vegetable oil in a browning dish and heat on full power for 2 minutes.

☛ Add the onion, red (bell) pepper, garlic and tomatoes. Stir round in the hot oil and cook on full power for 5 minutes.

☛ Drain the water from the beans and season well with salt and pepper. Add the pepper mixture and mix well.

☛ Sprinkle with chopped sage or basil, cover and cook for a further 5 minutes. Allow to stand for 2–3 minutes.

Mushroom Paté

INGREDIENTS

SERVES 4

4 cups/225 g/8 oz mushroom caps, washed

¼ cup/3 tbsp chopped parsley

2 garlic cloves

½ cup/50 g/2 oz fresh breadcrumbs

½ cup/50 g/2 oz grated cheese

¼ tsp ground nutmeg

¼ cup/50 g/2 oz butter

1 lemon, juice

1 tbsp Cognac

3 tbsp/2 tbsp double (thick) cream

parsley or chervil for garnish

PREPARATION

☛ Wash and slice the mushrooms finely and dry in absorbent paper towels.

☛ Wash and chop the parsley, peel and crush the garlic.

☛ Melt the butter in the browning dish in the microwave oven and add the garlic. Microwave on full power for 1 minute then remove and add the mushrooms. Stir, and cook on full power for a further 5 minutes.

☛ Add the parsley, breadcrumbs, cheese, nutmeg, seasoning, lemon juice, Cognac and cream to the mushrooms. Stir well and microwave for a further 1 minute on full power.

☛ Blend all the ingredients in the food processor or blender and turn into a bowl to set. Allow to cool before chilling in the refrigerator for 1 hour.

TO SERVE

Place in an attractive serving dish and accompany with crisp fingers of toast. Garnish with sprigs of parsley or any other available fresh herbs.

Courgette (Zucchini) and Bean Salad

INGREDIENTS

SERVES 4

4 courgettes (zucchini), washed

salt

1 tbsp lemon juice

1 red (bell) pepper, deseeded

½ lb/225 g/8 oz tender young green beans

2 spring onions (scallions)

2 cups/225 g/8 oz cherry tomatoes or
2 tomatoes, quartered

½ cup/125 ml/4 fl oz olive oil

3 tbsp/2 tbsp wine vinegar

pepper

1 tsp French mustard

1 tsp chopped tarragon

PREPARATION

☛ Cut the courgettes (zucchini) into slices and arrange in a casserole. Add ½ cup/125 ml/4 fl oz salted water and cook on full power for 3 minutes. Drain, retaining the water, and turn into a salad bowl. Sprinkle with lemon juice.

☛ Cut the (bell) pepper into strips and blanch in the courgette (zucchini) water on full power for 2 minutes. Remove to the bowl, retaining the water.

☛ Top and tail the beans, cut them in half and cook in the same water, covered, for 7 minutes. Drain the beans and arrange them in the bowl with the courgettes (zucchini) and (bell) peppers.

☛ Chop the spring onions (scallions) finely and sprinkle over the vegetables. Arrange the tomatoes on top to decorate.

☛ Mix oil, vinegar, salt, pepper, mustard and tarragon in a screw-top jar to make a dressing. Shake well and pour over the salad.

Chill for 20 minutes before serving.

VARIATION

Surround the salad with watercress. Add four hard-boiled (hard-cooked) eggs.

Hummus

INGREDIENTS

SERVES 4
2 cups/225 g/8 oz chick peas (garbanzos)
1 bouquet garni
1 small onion, peeled
2 garlic cloves, peeled
2 lemons, juice
2 tbsp/50 g/2 oz tahini paste
4 tbsp olive oil
salt
freshly ground pepper
1 tbsp parsley
1 tomato, sliced

PREPARATION

☛ Soak the chick peas for at least 6 hours and then drain them.

☛ Place the chick peas (garbanzos) in a large dish with 1 qt/1 L/1¾ pt water, bouquet garni and the sliced onion. Microwave for 20 minutes on full power. Leave to stand for 5 minutes, and then cook for a further 25 minutes, or until the peas are cooked and soft. Drain and allow to cool.

☛ Put all the other ingredients except the parsley in a blender or food processor. Gradually add the chick peas to the other ingredients until they make a smooth paste. Taste for seasoning.

☛ Arrange the hummus in a dish, and sprinkle with a little extra olive oil.

TO SERVE

Garnish with a sprig of parsley and tomato slices and serve with warm pitta (pita) bread.

Mushrooms à la Grecque

INGREDIENTS

SERVES 4

2 lemons, rind and juice

1 bouquet garni

1 bay leaf

6 peppercorns, slightly crushed

1 small onion, thinly sliced

¼ tsp soy sauce

6 cups/450 g/1 lb button mushrooms

½ cup/125 ml/4 fl oz white wine (optional)

freshly ground black pepper

PREPARATION

☛ Thinly peel the zest from one lemon and add to 1 cup/225 ml/8 fl oz water with the bouquet garni, bay leaf, peppercorns, onion and soy sauce.

☛ Microwave for 10 minutes at full power. Allow to stand for 10 minutes to infuse.

☛ Squeeze the juice of 1 lemon. Peel the other lemon and cut the flesh into thin slices. Wash the mushrooms and remove the stalks.

☛ Arrange the mushrooms in a microwave dish. Strain the stock over the mushrooms. Cover with the lemon juice, wine and thin slices of lemon, and add a dash of ground black pepper. Microwave at full power for 6 minutes, allow to stand for 5 minutes and then cook at full power for a further 6 minutes. Allow to cool.

☛ Sprinkle with chopped parsley, pour 1 tbsp olive oil over the mushrooms and chill.

VARIATION

LEEKS À LA GRECQUE

Substitute trimmed and sliced leeks for the mushrooms. Cook as above.

ARTICHOKES À LA GRECQUE

Small, young tender artichokes may be trimmed, choke removed and prepared in this way. If using canned or frozen artichoke hearts, reduce the cooking time by half.

LEFT: *Artichokes à la Grecque*

Spicy Stuffed Courgettes (Zucchini)

INGREDIENTS

SERVES 4–6

6 courgettes (zucchini), washed

salt

1 tbsp lemon juice

½ cup/100 g/4 oz long grain rice, washed

1 onion, peeled and diced

1 red (bell) pepper, deseeded and diced

½ cup/125 ml/4 fl oz vegetable oil

1 garlic clove, crushed

2 tomatoes, skinned

1 tsp curry powder

1 cup/100 g/4 oz mushrooms, washed

pepper

⅔ cup/150 ml/¼ pt sour cream

1 tsp paprika

1 tbsp chopped parsley or coriander

PREPARATION

☛ Cut the courgettes (zucchini) lengthwise and arrange them in a flat dish with ½ cup/125 ml/4 fl oz salted water. Cover and microwave on full power for 4 minutes. Drain and sprinkle with lemon juice.

☛ Place the washed rice in a casserole with 1½ cups/ 350 ml/12 fl oz water mixed with ½ teaspoon salt. Cook on full power for 8 minutes and then allow to stand for 3 minutes or until the rice has absorbed the water. If it hasn't, cook for a further 2 minutes.

☛ Mix the onion and (bell) peppers with three-quarters of the oil and the crushed garlic. Cook on full power for 4 minutes before stirring in the chopped tomatoes, the curry powder and chopped mushrooms.

☛ Scoop out the inside of the courgettes (zucchini) with a small knife. Chop the flesh and add to vegetable mixture. Cook on full power for 4 minutes, stir well and season with salt and pepper.

☛ Mix the rice with the vegetable mixture and half of the sour cream and taste for seasoning.

☛ Brush the courgettes (zucchini) with oil inside and out and spoon the stuffing into the shells. Arrange in a flat oiled dish and cook on full power for 5 minutes, and then on half power for 5 minutes. Cook in two batches if the courgettes (zucchini) are large.

TO SERVE

Sprinkle each halved courgette (zucchini) with the remaining cream, a little paprika and chopped parsley or coriander. This dish can be served hot or cold.

Autumn Dishes

RIGHT: *Thai Rice*

Thai Rice

INGREDIENTS

SERVES 4

2⅓ cups/450 g/1 lb long grain rice

1 tsp salt

1 tsp turmeric

¼ cup/50 ml/2 fl oz vegetable oil

2 garlic cloves, crushed

2 onions, peeled and diced

1 chilli (chili) pepper, deseeded

1 red (bell) pepper, deseeded

1 tsp curry powder

2 spring onions (scallions)

2 cups/225 g/8 oz peas

2 eggs

salt and pepper

1 tsp soy sauce

1 tbsp/15 g/½ oz butter

PREPARATION

☛ Wash the long grain rice and put in a large casserole with 1 qt/1 L/1¾ pt boiling water with the salt and turmeric. Cook on full power for 15 minutes and then allow to stand. The rice should be fluffy and separated.

☛ Heat the oil in a dish for 1 minute on full power, add the garlic and cook for a further 1 minute. Add the onion, stir well and cook for 2 minutes.

☛ Dice both the peppers, add them to the garlic and onion and cook for 2 minutes. Stir in the curry powder with half of the chopped spring onion (scallions), mix with the rice and stir in the peas.

☛ Make up an omelette (omelet) mixture by beating 2 eggs, 2 tbsp water, seasoning and soy sauce in a bowl. Put the butter into a browning dish and heat on full power for 1 minute. Stir in the eggs and cook on full power for 1 minute and remove.

☛ Mix to allow any uncooked mixture to run under the cooked egg. Cook on high, for another 1 minute, allow to stand for 30 seconds and remove to a chopping board.

☛ Reheat the rice for 4 minutes on full power.

TO SERVE

Cut the omelette (omelet) into strips and use it to decorate the top of the rice. Sprinkle with chopped spring onion (scallion).

Stuffed Mushrooms

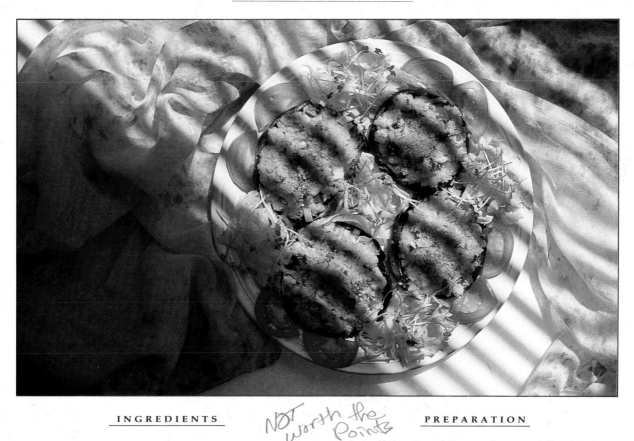

INGREDIENTS

NOT worth the points

SERVES 4

4/6 ~~12~~ large open (cup) mushrooms ⌀	
1 ~~2~~ tbsp/25 g/2 oz butter 3	
1 onion, chopped ⌀	
2 tomatoes, skinned ⌀	
¼ ⅓ cup/50 g/2 oz raisins 3	
¼ cup/25 g/1 oz (pine nuts) almonds 6	
½ 1 cup/50 g/2 oz fresh breadcrumbs 3	
1 tbsp parsley, chopped ⌀	
salt and pepper ⌀	
1 egg 1	
1 tsp paprika ⌀	

4/16/8

PREPARATION

☛ Cut off the tips of the mushroom stalks, leaving a little piece of stalk in the mushroom as this helps to hold them together. Chop the remaining stalks.

☛ Melt 1 tbsp/25 g/1 oz butter on full power for 1 minute. Add the onion and mushroom stalks, cook on full for 2 minutes.

☛ Chop the tomatoes, add them to the onion mixture and cook for a further 1 minute on full power.

☛ Mix in all the other ingredients except the paprika and mix with the beaten egg. Pile the mixture onto the mushroom caps. Brush with melted butter.

☛ Arrange half the mushroom caps on a buttered dish and cook, covered, for 3 minutes on full power, pause for 1 minute and continue cooking for another 3 minutes. Keep warm while the remainder of the mushrooms are cooked.

TO SERVE

Sprinkle with a little paprika. These mushrooms can be sliced and served cold with salad.

Garlic Mushrooms

INGREDIENTS

SERVES 4
¼ cup/50 g/2 oz butter
2 garlic cloves, crushed
6 cups/450 g/1 lb mushrooms
1 lemon, juice
1 tbsp chopped parsley
salt and pepper
¼ cup/50 ml/2 fl oz single cream (half-and-half)
¼ tsp paprika

PREPARATION

☛ Heat the butter in a large dish for 1 minute on full power. Add the garlic and cook for a further 1 minute.
☛ Dry the mushrooms with kitchen towels. Trim the tips of the stalks where necessary. Add the mushrooms to the butter and garlic, stir well and cook uncovered for 3 minutes on full power.
☛ Add the lemon juice, half the parsley and seasoning. Cook for a further 2 minutes on full power.

TO SERVE

Sprinkle with single cream (half-and-half), chopped parsley and the paprika.

Corn on the Cob

INGREDIENTS

SERVES 4
4 corn on the cob with husks
4 tbsp/50 g/2 oz butter
1 tbsp green or black olives, stoned (pitted) and sliced
1 tsp capers, chopped
2 spring onions (scallions) chopped
½ red (bell) pepper, deseeded and diced
½ cup/50 g/2 oz mushrooms, washed and sliced
salt and freshly ground pepper

PREPARATION

☛ Microwave the corn in the husks with ½ cup/125 ml/4 fl oz water, covered, for 5 minutes. Allow to stand for 2 minutes.

☛ Melt the butter in a bowl on full power for 1 minute. Add all the other ingredients and cook for 3 minutes.

☛ Remove the husks from the corn. Pour the butter mixture over the corn. Season well.

Beetroot (Beets) in Onion Sauce

INGREDIENTS

SERVES 4

2 tbsp/25 g/1 oz butter

1 onion, peeled

1 garlic clove

1 lemon, rind grated, juice squeezed

½ tsp paprika

2½ cups/600 ml/1 pt Béchamel Sauce (see page 19)

6 cups/700 g/1½ lb cooked beetroot (beets), sliced

¼ cup/50 ml/2 fl oz heavy cream (optional)

1 tbsp chopped parsley or chopped chives

PREPARATION

☛ In a microwave dish melt the butter on full power for 1 minute. Add the diced onion and crushed garlic and cook for 3 minutes or until the onion is transparent. Grate the rind of the lemon and squeeze the juice.

☛ Make the Béchamel Sauce, season well and add the lemon rind with the paprika.

☛ Add the beetroot (beets) to the onion mixture and sprinkle with lemon juice. Cook, covered, for 5 minutes. Pour over the Béchamel Sauce.

TO SERVE

Drizzle the cream over the beetroot (beets) and sprinkle with chopped parsley or chives.

Note If you cannot get precooked beetroot (beets), cook them covered with water in the microwave oven for 10 minutes on full power. Turn them and cook for a further 10 minutes.

Baked Potatoes

INGREDIENTS

SERVES 4

4 large baking potatoes

PREPARATION

☛ Wash the potatoes thoroughly and prick the skins with a fork.

☛ Cook on full power for 20 minutes, then allow to stand for 5 minutes. Test with a fork: the cooking time will depend on the size of the potatoes. One potato will take 5–7 minutes depending on size but several will, of course, take longer.

BAKED POTATOES WITH SOUR CREAM AND CHIVES

Halve the cooked potatoes and scoop out the centre into a bowl. Mix with 1 cup/225 ml/8 fl oz sour cream and 2 tbsp chives. Season well with salt and freshly ground pepper. Mix and replace the filling. Reheat in the microwave for 4 minutes on full power.

BAKED POTATOES WITH VEGETABLE CHILLI (CHILI)

Halve the cooked potatoes and scoop out a little of the centre. Mix the potato with the vegetable chilli (chili) (see page 107), refill the potatoes and reheat for 5 minutes on full power.

BAKED POTATO NESTS

Halve the cooked potatoes, scoop out the flesh into a bowl. Mix with ½ cup/50 g/2 oz grated cheese, 2–3 tbsp milk, salt and freshly ground pepper and 2 tsp chives. Cream the mixture together until fluffy. Fill the potatoes; make a hollow in each potato with the back of a tablespoon. Brush with melted butter. Break 1 egg for each halved potato into a cup and slip into the hollow. Prick the yolk with a sterilized skewer or large needle. Return four potato nests to the microwave and cook on full for 2 minutes, and stand for 2 minutes. Cook the other four half potatoes and serve with a green vegetable for a most substantial meal.

SAUCY BAKED POTATOES

Make 1¼ cups/300 ml/½ pt Cheese Sauce (see page 19). Chop 1 cup/100 g/4 oz mushrooms finely and mix with the Cheese Sauce. Cut a thin slice from the top of each potato, scoop out some of the flesh and squash rest of the potato in its skin. Fill with mushroom sauce, top with a slice of cheese and reheat for 5 minutes on full power.

Spinach and Mushroom Mould

INGREDIENTS

SERVES 4

2 lb/1 kg/2 lb fresh spinach, chopped or
1 lb/450 g/1 lb frozen chopped spinach

2 tbsp/25 g/1 oz butter

2 cups/225 g/8 oz mushrooms, washed

½ tsp grated nutmeg

salt and pepper

1¼ cups/300 ml/½ pt Béchamel Sauce (see page 19)

¼ lb/100 g/4 oz mozzarella cheese

PREPARATION

☛ Cook the chopped spinach in the microwave oven for 5 minutes, covered, on full power. If using frozen spinach, defrost it.

☛ Melt the butter and add the sliced mushrooms. Stir and cook for another 1 minute on full power.

☛ In a buttered, rectangular dish or microwave ring mold (tube pan) arrange one layer of the drained spinach, season well, and drizzle a spoonful of the Béchamel Sauce over the surface. Arrange a layer of sliced mushrooms and then a layer of sliced Mozzarella cheese. Continue layering until all the ingredients are used, reserving half of the Béchamel Sauce.

☛ Cook on full power for 5 minutes and then allow to stand for 2 minutes. Finish cooking at full power for a further 5 minutes.

☛ Unmould (unmold) if using a ring mold (tube pan). Reheat the sauce in the microwave oven for 2 minutes on full power and whisk to ensure that it is smooth.

TO SERVE

Pour the heated suace over the Spinach and Mushroom Mould (Mold).

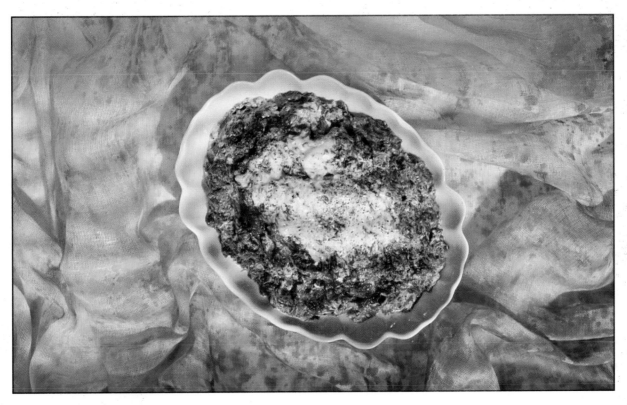

Creamed Spinach

INGREDIENTS

SERVES 4

2 lb/1 kg/2 lb fresh spinach or
12 oz/350 g/12 oz frozen spinach

½ tsp salt

2 tbsp/25 g/1 oz butter

2 tbsp/25 g/1 oz flour

freshly ground pepper

freshly grated nutmeg

½ cup/125 ml/4 fl oz single cream (half-and-half)

PREPARATION

☛ Prepare fresh spinach, if using, by removing the thick stalks and tear the leaves into strips. Cook at full power with ⅔ cup/150 ml/¼ pt salted water for 3 minutes. Drain through a sieve, reserving the water. Defrost the frozen spinach, if using.

☛ Melt the butter in a browning dish for 1 minute, add the flour and stir well. Pour in the liquid from the spinach, season with pepper and nutmeg and mix well. Microwave on full power for 1 minute, remove and whisk briskly.

☛ Gradually beat in the cream and return to the microwave for a further 1 minute on full power. Remove and whisk again until smooth.

☛ Add the cooked spinach and mix well. Reheat on full power for 3 minutes or until heated through.

Mushroom Moussaka

INGREDIENTS

SERVES 4

---

2 aubergines (eggplants)

---

salt

---

1 lemon, juice

½ lb/225 g/8 oz mushrooms

---

4 tomatoes, skinned

2½ cups/600 ml/1 pt Béchamel Sauce (see page 19)

¼ cup/50 g/2 oz butter

---

2 tbsp vegetable oil

---

1 onion, peeled

---

1 garlic clove, crushed

---

pepper

---

1 tsp soy sauce

---

1 cup/100 g/4 oz grated cheese

½ cup/25 g/1 oz fresh breadcrumbs

PREPARATION

☛ Slice the aubergines (eggplant) lengthwise and sprinkle with a little salt and lemon juice. Stand for 20 minutes, cut side down, to allow the bitter juices to drain out.

☛ Chop the mushrooms, including the trimmed stalks. Slice the tomatoes.

☛ Make up the Béchamel Sauce, making sure that it is well seasoned.

☛ Melt the butter at full power for 1 minute in a dish large enough for the moussaka.

☛ Drain the aubergines (eggplant) and dry with kitchen towels. Lay the slices in the warmed butter (this may take 2–3 batches depending on the size of the dish). Cook each batch on full power for 4 minutes wth 1–2 minutes standing time. Three batches may require a little more butter.

☛ Leave the last batch in the bottom of the dish and sprinkle with seasoning.

☛ Pour the oil into another dish. Cook the diced onion and crushed garlic at full power for 2 minutes. Add the mushrooms and cook on full power for 2 minutes. Season with salt, pepper and soy sauce.

☛ Spread some of the mushroom mixture over the first layer of aubergines (eggplant) and top with slices of tomato. Pour over a third of the sauce and sprinkle with cheese. Continue with the layers until all the ingredients are used. Top with Béchamel Sauce and sprinkle with a mixture of breadcrumbs and cheese.

☛ Cook uncovered on full power for 10 minutes; allow to stand for 2 minutes, then cook for a further 5 minutes.

TO SERVE

Place under a hot grill (broiler) until cheese and crumbs brown. Or add a sliced tomato before returning the dish to the oven for the last 5 minutes of cooking time.

Oriental Rice

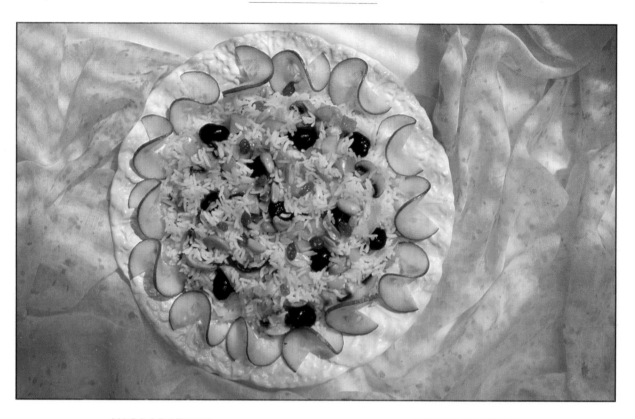

INGREDIENTS

SERVES 4

1 cup/200 g/7 oz long grain rice
salt
½ cup/50 g/2 oz small mushrooms
2 dessert apples
1 tbsp wine vinegar
1 large onion, finely chopped (minced)
1 tbsp vegetable oil
⅓ cup/50 g/2 oz sultanas
½ cup/50 g/2 oz cashew nuts
½ cup/50 g/2 oz salted peanuts
20 black olives (pitted)
1 tbsp/15 g/½ oz curry powder

PREPARATION

☛ Wash the rice until the water runs clear. Put it into a very large container with 3¾ cups/850 ml/1½ pt water and salt. Microwave, uncovered, on full power for 15 minutes. Rinse and leave to drain thoroughly.

☛ Slice the mushrooms, chop the apples leaving the skins on. Put the chopped apple in a bowl with the vinegar.

☛ Put the oil in a large bowl and heat for 2 minutes on full power. Add the onion, stir and cover with a plate or pierced cling film (plastic wrap) and microwave on full power for 3 minutes.

☛ Combine all the ingredients, season to taste and cook on full power for 4 minutes stirring after 2 minutes. Serve with a green salad.

Fruit Chutney

INGREDIENTS

MAKES 6×1 LB/450 G/1 LB JARS
2¼ lb/1 kg/2¼ lb apples, peeled, cored and sliced
2¼ lb/1 kg/2¼ lb onions, peeled and sliced
2 lemons, rind grated, juice squeezed
½ cup/100 g/4 oz dried apricots, chopped
6 cups/700 g/1½ lb brown sugar
2½ cups/600 ml/1 pt malt vinegar
1 small green chilli (chili) pepper, deseeded
1⅓ cup/225 g/8 oz sultanas (yellow raisins)
1⅓ cups/225 g/8 oz raisins

PREPARATION

☛ In a large bowl, microwave the sliced apples and onion rings, covered, for 5 minutes on full power.

☛ Add the lemon rind and juice, stir them and then add the apricots and sugar. Mix well.

☛ Cook for 10 minutes on full power, stirring to dissolve the sugar. When it is dissolved, add the vinegar, chopped chilli (chili) pepper, sultanas (yellow raisins) and raisins.

☛ Cook uncovered for 1–1½ hours until thick. Ladle into sterilized jars, seal and label.

Mango Chutney

INGREDIENTS

2 (about 750 g/1½ lb) mangoes, peeled and diced

1 large onion, chopped

⅓ cup/50 g/2 oz raisins

⅓ cup/50 g/2 oz dried apricots, chopped

1 tbsp rum

1¼ cups/300 ml/½ pint wine or cider vinegar

sugar

½ tsp allspice

½ cinnamon stick

1 piece of ginger

1 small green chilli (chili) pepper, deseeded

PREPARATION

☞ Mix the onion with the mangoes and cover with 1¼ cups/300 ml/½ pt of water in a large bowl. Cook on full power for 5 minutes.

☞ Soak the raisins and apricots in the rum.

☞ Drain the mangoes and weigh the fruit. Use the same weight of fruit as sugar for the chutney.

☞ Pour the vinegar into a jug and add the sugar and spices. Microwave on full power for 4 minutes to melt the sugar. Check to see if sugar is completely dissolved and if not, cook for a further 2 minutes.

☞ Return the mangoes to the bowl with the vinegar and sugar mixture and stir in the raisins, apricots and chopped chilli (chili). Cook at full power for 10 minutes and then stand for 5 minutes. Cook for a further 10 minutes on full power or until the mixture becomes thick.

☞ To test it, put a spoonful on a cold plate, leave to cool and see if it wrinkles when pushed. If the mixture is still too runny, cook for another 2–3 minutes.

☞ Bottle in sterilized jars. Seal and label.

TO SERVE

This chutney is an excellent accompaniment to spicy dishes and curries. It can also be served with vegetarian cutlets and nut roasts.

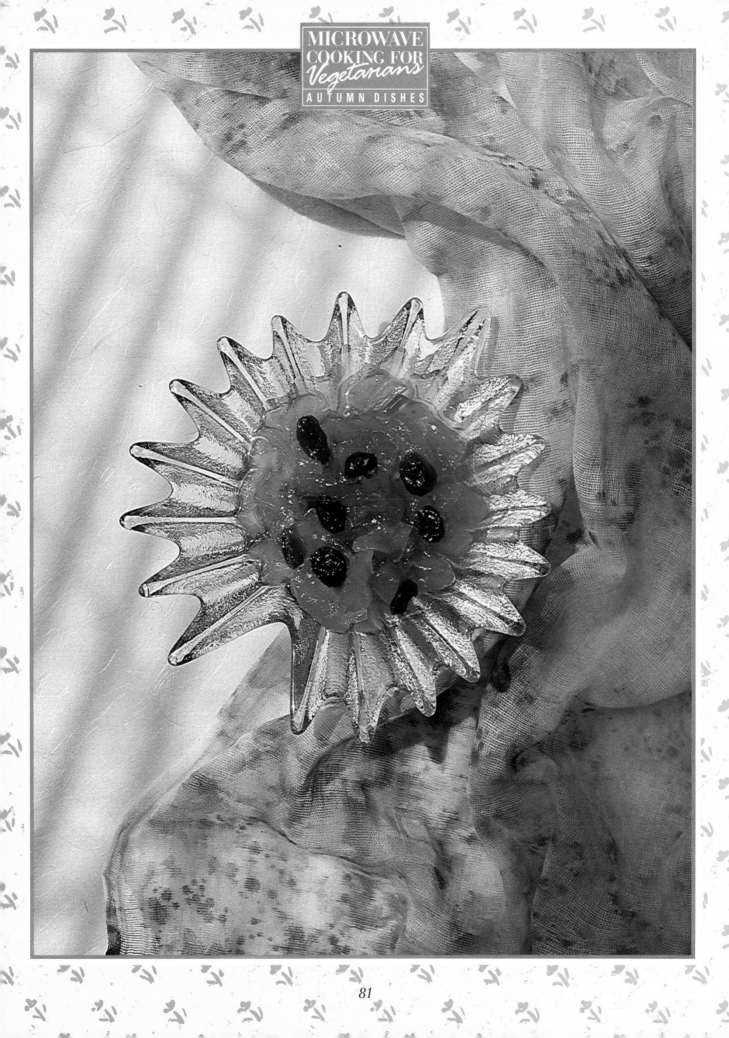

Rosemary and Apple Jelly

INGREDIENTS

MAKES 3 LB/2.25 KG/3 LB
8 cups/1 kg/2 lb cooking (tart) apples, sliced
3 tbsp/2 tbsp rosemary
3 black peppercorns, lightly crushed
1 cup/225 ml/8 fl oz wine or cider vinegar
about 5 cups/1 kg/2 lb sugar
2–3 drops green vegetable colouring (optional)

PREPARATION

☞ Place the apples in a casserole or large bowl with half the rosemary, ½ cup/125 ml/4 fl oz water and the peppercorns. Cook on full power for 15 minutes. By this time the apples should be fairly soft.

☞ Add the vinegar and cook on full power for a further 10 minutes. Allow to cool slightly; push through a nylon sieve. Measure the liquid and add 1 lb/450 g/1 lb sugar for every 2½ cups/600 ml/1 pt of apple and rosemary purée.

☞ Melt the sugar by microwaving on full power for 5 minutes. Remove and stir, and then return to the microwave on full power for a further 5 minutes to make sure that the sugar is dissolved. Cook on full power for 15 minutes. Add the remaining rosemary and the green colouring, if using. Test for setting on a cold plate. If the jelly wrinkles in 1 minute, it is ready to pot; if not, cook for a further 5 minutes.

☞ Pour into sterilized jars and seal. Label with the date.

TO SERVE

This jelly is delicious with cooked vegetables.

Poached Fruit

INGREDIENTS

SERVES 4

4 peaches, pitted and sliced

2 tbsp/25 g/1 oz soft brown sugar

1 lemon, juice squeezed

PREPARATION

☛ Arrange the peach slices in a microwave baking dish.

☛ Stir the sugar and lemon juice into 1 cup/225 ml/ 8 fl oz water and heat for 2 minutes at full power.

☛ Pour onto the peaches and cook at full power for 4 minutes.

TO SERVE

The fruit can either be drained and served with a butterscotch sauce or with whipped cream.

VARIATION

COOKING (TART) APPLES

Peel and slice 1½ lb/700 g/1½ lb apples. Poach them in the syrup with 1 extra tbsp sugar for 8 minutes on full power. Add cloves or cinnamon for extra taste.

PEARS

Peel 4 pears, remove the cores and cook in the syrup for 10 minutes on full power.

PLUMS

Wash, halve and stone 12 plums. Cook in the syrup for 4 minutes.

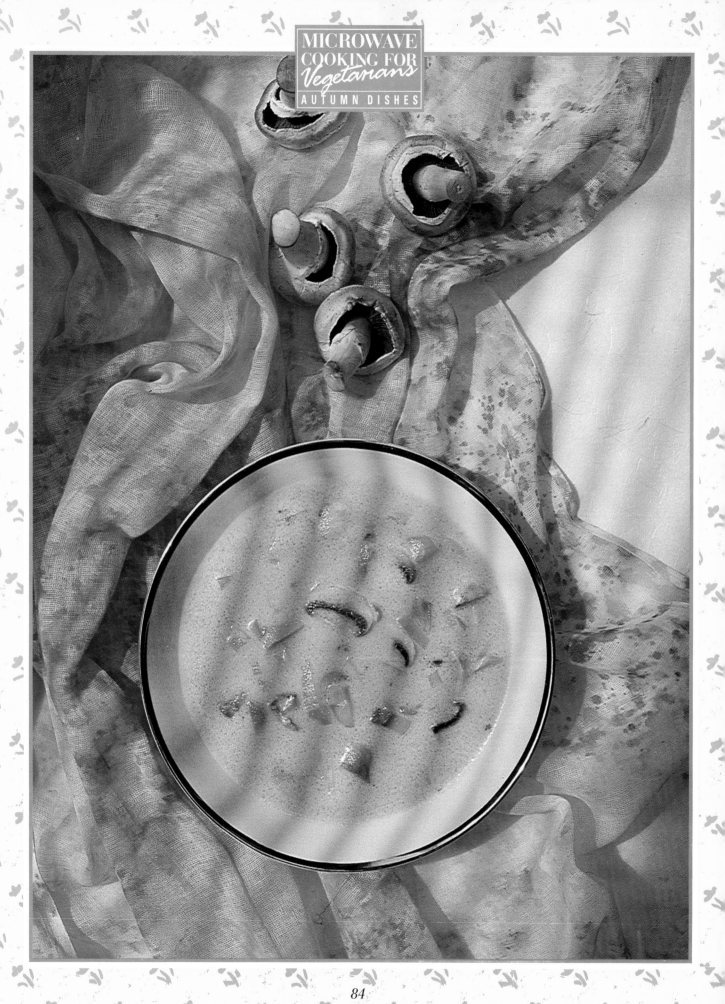

Mushroom Soup

INGREDIENTS

SERVES 4
2 tbsp/25 g/1 oz butter
1 onion, peeled and chopped
1 garlic clove, crushed
6 cups/450 g/1 lb mushrooms, washed
¼ cup/25 g/1 oz flour
2½ cups/600 ml/1 pt vegetable stock
½ tsp thyme
1 bay leaf
2 sprigs of parsley
¼ cup/50 ml/2 fl oz single cream (half-and-half)

PREPARATION

☞ Melt the butter in a large casserole or bowl for 2 minutes.

☞ Add the onion and garlic and cook on full power for 2 minutes.

☞ Slice the mushrooms finely and chop the stalks separately. Add to the onion, cook on full power for 3 minutes. Stir and cook for a further 2 minutes.

☞ Remove from the microwave oven and stir in the flour until it has mixed well with any remaining butter. Add half the vegetable stock, stir well and cook for 5 minutes at full.

☞ Mix the thyme, bay leaf and parsley with the remaining stock and pour the mixture over the mushrooms. Season well and cook on full power for a further 10 minutes. Allow to stand for 5 minutes and remove the herbs.

TO SERVE

Stir in the cream. The soup can be liquidized if you prefer a smoother texture.

Cheese Soufflé

INGREDIENTS

SERVES 6
¼ cup/50 g/2 oz butter
1¼ cups/300 ml/½ pt milk
¼ cup/25 g/1 oz plain (all purpose) flour
½ tsp mustard
¼ tsp cayenne pepper
salt and freshly ground pepper
1 cup/100 g/4 oz grated Cheddar cheese
4 eggs
2 tsp Parmesan cheese
1 tbsp chopped parsley

PREPARATION

☞ Place the butter in a large soufflé dish, cook on full power for 1 minute. Remove from the oven, replace with the milk in a jug. Heat on full power for 2 minutes. Stir the flour into the melted butter to make a smooth paste.

☞ Add the warm milk to the roux of flour and butter, whisk well to form a smooth mixture. Add the mustard, cayenne and seasoning. Cook on full power for 2 minutes, whisk again and cook for a further 2 minutes until the sauce is thick.

☞ Add the grated Cheddar cheese and whisk in the egg yolks until the mixture is smooth.

☞ Whisk the egg whites just until they form soft peaks. Fold the egg whites into the mixture in the soufflé dish with a plastic spatula.

☞ Cook on low power for 25 minutes.

TO SERVE

Sprinkle with Parmesan cheese and parsley. Serve immediately with a salad or crisp green vegetables.

LEFT: *Mushroom Soup*

Spicy Rice

INGREDIENTS

SERVES 4–8

2⅓ cups/450 g/1 lb long grain rice

¼ cup/50 g/2 oz butter

½ cup/125 ml/4 fl oz oil

1 onion, chopped

1 garlic clove

6 cloves

1 cinnamon stick

6 cardamom pods

½ tsp turmeric

1 tsp salt

1 qt/1 L/1¼ pt vegetable stock

¾ cup/75 g/3 oz slivered almonds

⅔ cup/100 g/4 oz sultanas

1 spring onion (scallion) or
1 tbsp chopped coriander

PREPARATION

☛ Wash the long grain rice several times in cold running water. Allow to drain well and pat dry with kitchen towels.

☛ Heat the butter and oil in a large casserole or pyrex bowl on full power for 2 minutes or until it starts to foam. Add the onion quickly and cook on full power for 3 minutes.

☛ Add the crushed garlic and the other spices. Stir, and cook on full power for 1 minute.

☛ Remove from the oven and stir in the rice, making sure each grain is coated with oil and butter. Return to the microwave and cook for 2 minutes. Add the stock, cover the dish with a lid or cling film (plastic wrap). Pierce the cling film (plastic wrap) and cook until all the liquid is absorbed.

☛ Fry the slivered almonds in a few drops of oil in a frying pan (skillet) on the stove top until golden. Remove the cinnamon stick and as many cloves and cardamom pods from the rice as you can find.

☛ Mix the almonds and sultanas with the rice. Sprinkle with finely chopped spring onions (scallions) or coriander. This dish can be served hot with curry or cold with dressing as part of a starter or salad.

Baked Sweet Peppers

INGREDIENTS

SERVES 4

2 large sweet peppers, deseeded and halved

1 large onion, peeled and diced

1 cup/100 g/4 oz mushrooms, diced

2 tbsp/25 g/1 oz butter

1¼ cups/300 ml/½ pt Béchamel (White) Sauce
(see page 19)

salt and pepper

4 slices cheese

PREPARATION

☛ Place the peppers in a covered dish with ¼ cup/50 ml/2 fl oz water and cook on full power for 5 minutes. Drain on a wire rack.

☛ Cook the onion and mushrooms in butter for 4 minutes.

☛ Prepare the Béchamel Sauce, mix it with the mushrooms and onion and season well.

☛ Stuff the peppers with the mushroom sauce and cook for 5 minutes at full power.

☛ Top with slices of cheese and cook for a further 2 minutes.

VARIATION

Cook 1 extra diced pepper with the onions and mushrooms. Mix with 1 cup/8 tbsp cooked rice, seasoning and 1 tbsp chopped parsley. Stuff the sweet peppers. Serve with Tomato Sauce (see page 15) or top with cheese as preferred.

Parsnip and Apple Soup

INGREDIENTS

SERVES 4
2 tbsp/1 oz/25 g butter
1 onion, diced
4 cups/450 g/1 lb parsnips, diced
½ lb/225 g/8 oz cooking apples
1 tsp mixed herbs
1 qt/1 L/1¾ pt vegetable stock
1 cup/225 ml/8 fl oz single (half-and-half) cream
1 tbsp chopped parsley

PREPARATION

☛ Melt the butter in a browning dish for 2 minutes. Add the onion to the melted butter and cook on full power for 2 minutes.
☛ Add the parsnips to the onion and cook on full power for 3 minutes. Add the sliced apple and herbs and cook for a further 2 minutes.
☛ Pour on the stock and cook, covered, for 10 minutes on full power. Allow to stand for a few minutes.
☛ Put the soup in a blender or liquidizer, add the cream and reheat for 5 minutes.

TO SERVE

Sprinkle with chopped parsley and serve with wholemeal (wholewheat) bread.

Winter Dishes

RIGHT: *Creamed Brussels Sprouts*

Creamed Brussels Sprouts

INGREDIENTS

SERVES 4

1 lb/700 g/1½ lb Brussels sprouts, washed and trimmed

½ cup/125 ml/4 fl oz cream

salt and freshly ground pepper

1 small can whole chestnuts

PREPARATION

☞ Place the sprouts in a deep dish with 1 cup/225 ml/8 fl oz water, cover and cook on full power for 10 minutes. Allow to stand for 3 minutes and then test them: for this recipe the sprouts need to be less crunchy than when being used whole. If they are still too crisp, cook for a further 3 minutes and then drain.

☞ Purée the sprouts in a food processor or large blender, adding the cream, salt and pepper. Pour the purée into a microwave dish.

☞ Add the chestnuts, return to the microwave oven and re-heat for 5 minutes.

Creamy Orzo Risotto with Butternut Squash

Weight Watchers Recipe

★ ★ ★ ★ ☆

Course: main meals
PointsPlus® Value: 6
Servings: 4
Preparation Time: 15 min
Cooking Time: 25 min
Level of Difficulty: Easy

So rich and creamy! A wonderful, light take on classic butternut squash risotto. Thyme sprigs give great flavor but feel free to substitute sage leaves instead.

Ingredients

1 spray(s) cooking spray
2 cup(s) uncooked butternut squash, cut into small cubes
1/2 tsp olive oil
1/8 tsp table salt, or to taste
1/2 Tbsp unsalted butter
1 cup(s) uncooked orzo
1 1/2 cup(s) water
1 cup(s) canned chicken broth
1 tsp thyme, fresh, fresh, or 8 whole sprigs (sprigs preferred)
2 Tbsp fat-free half-and-half
1/3 cup(s) grated Parmesan cheese, such as Parmigiano-Reggiano
1/8 tsp table salt, or to taste
1/8 tsp black pepper, freshly ground, or to taste

Instructions

Preheat oven to 425°F. Coat a small rimmed baking sheet with cooking spray.

In a medium bowl, toss squash with oil and salt; spread in a single layer on prepared baking sheet, leaving space between squash cubes. Roast, stirring halfway through, until squash is tender and lightly browned, about 20 to 25 minutes.

Meanwhile, melt butter in a medium saucepan over medium heat; add orzo. Stir constantly until orzo begins to smell toasty, about 3 minutes. Add water, broth and thyme sprigs; bring to a boil. Reduce heat to low; simmer, uncovered, stirring occasionally, until liquid is nearly absorbed, about 15 minutes.

Remove thyme sprigs; stir in half-and-half, cheese and roasted squash. Season well with salt and pepper; serve. Yields about 3/4 cup per serving.

Butter Bean and Mushroom Chowder

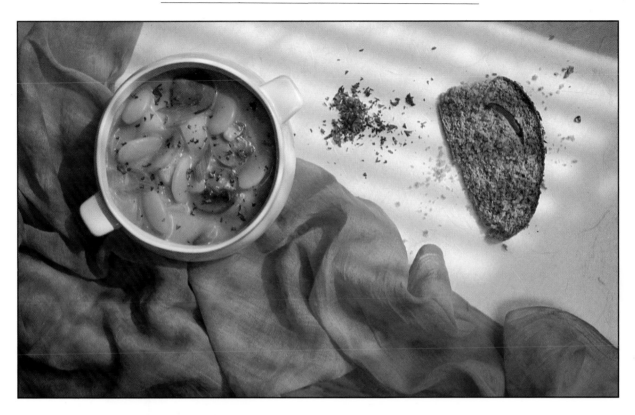

INGREDIENTS

SERVES 4

¼ lb/100 g/4 oz butter (lima) beans

2½ cups/600 ml/1 pt vegetable stock (broth)

2 onions, diced

2 stalks of celery, sliced

½ lb/225 g/8 oz potatoes, peeled and cubed

2 tbsp/25 g/1 oz butter

salt and pepper

¼ lb/100 g/4 oz mushrooms, sliced

1 small can sweet corn

1¼ cups/300 ml/½ pt milk

1 tbsp chopped parsley

wholemeal (wholewheat) bread

PREPARATION

☛ Soak the butter (lima) beans overnight in cold water. Pour the stock over the beans in a suitable casserole and cook at full power for 20 minutes.

☛ Melt the butter in a browning dish for 1 minute. Add the onions and celery for 2 minutes on full power. Add the potatoes, stir and cook for 2 minutes. Stir again, return to the microwave oven and cook for a further 3 minutes on full power.

☛ Mix the vegetables and beans and season well. Cook on full power for 10 minutes, stand for 5 minutes, then remove from the oven.

☛ Add the mushrooms and corn to the soup with the milk. Cook on full power for 10 minutes. Test the beans and potatoes. Should they be too crisp for your taste, cook on half power for up to a further 10 minutes.

☛ Remove from the microwave oven, taste for seasoning.

TO SERVE

Sprinkle with chopped parsley and serve with slices of wholemeal (wholewheat) bread.

Vegetable Soup with Spicy Sauce

INGREDIENTS

SERVES 6

3½ cups/750 g/12 oz haricot (navy) beans,
soaked overnight

¾ lb/750 g/12 oz ripe tomatoes

1 onion, peeled and diced

¼ cup/50 ml/2 fl oz vegetable oil

salt and pepper

1 tsp Worcestershire sauce

1 tsp dried mixed herbs

1 qt/1 L/1¾ pt vegetable stock (broth)

2 carrots, sliced

2¼ cups/350 g/12 oz peas

2 potatoes, peeled and sliced

1 leek, trimmed and sliced

¼ cup/50 g/2 oz butter

½ cup/50 g/2 oz flour

1 tbsp parsley

PREPARATION

☛ Put the beans into a bowl, cover them with water and microwave on full power for 10 minutes. Allow to stand for 2 minutes, then cook for a further 5 minutes.

☛ Place the tomatoes in a bowl with water and scald for 2 minutes at full power. Peel and slice the tomatoes. Add to the onion in a dish with the oil. Season with salt and pepper and cook for 2 minutes on full power.

☛ Add the Worcestershire sauce, mixed herbs and half of the stock (broth). Cook on full power for 5 minutes.

☛ Clean and prepare the rest of the vegetables. Just cover with the remaining vegetable stock and cook, with the beans, on full power for 15 minutes.

☛ Sieve the tomato mixture, collecting the purée in a bowl.

☛ Melt the butter for 1 minute on full power. Remove from the oven, add the flour and stir carefully. Mix until smooth with the tomato mixture and then cook for 5 minutes at full power, stirring well.

☛ Mix the tomato purée into the vegetable soup. Cook on full power for 10 minutes.

TO SERVE

Sprinkle with chopped parsley.

Lentil and Tomato Soup

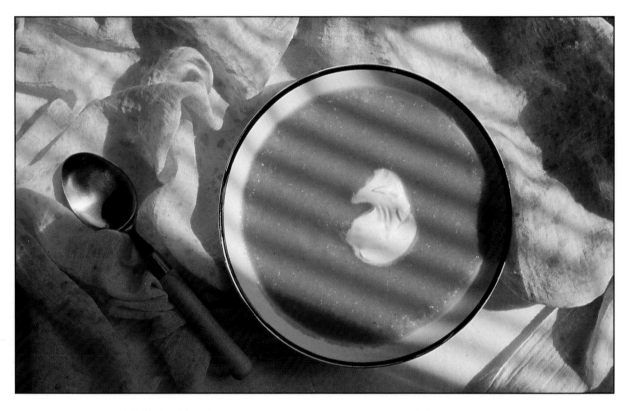

INGREDIENTS

SERVES 4

¼ lb/225 g/8 oz lentils

---

1 onion, peeled and diced

---

2 carrots, scraped and grated

2½ cups/600 ml/1 pt vegetable stock (broth)

---

1 bay leaf

---

1 bouquet garni

---

2 × 14 oz/400 g/14 oz cans tomatoes

---

1 tsp oregano

---

salt and pepper

¼ cup/50 ml/2 fl oz cream

PREPARATION

☛ Wash the lentils first with cold water and then with boiling water and remove any discoloured seeds.

☛ Put the lentils in a large bowl. Add the onion and carrots to the lentils and pour the stock (broth) over them. Cook on full power for 10 minutes. Allow to stand for 5 minutes. Then cook for a further 5 minutes at full power.

☛ Add all the remaining ingredients except the cream, including the juice from the tomatoes. Cook on full power for a further 15 minutes, remove and stir well. Allow to stand for 5 minutes.

☛ Purée in a blender or food processor and reheat as required.

TO SERVE

Spoon a little cream onto each bowl of soup before serving.

French Onion Soup

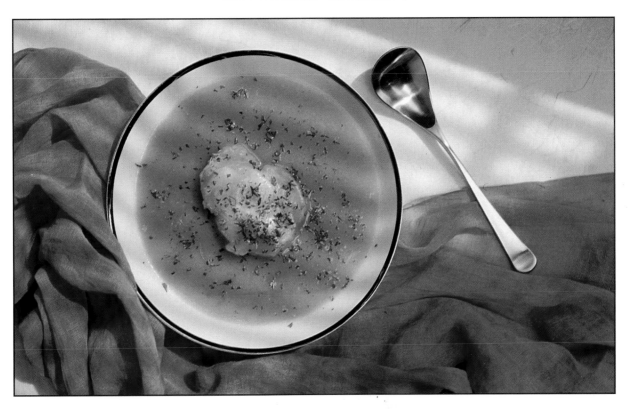

INGREDIENTS

SERVES 4
2 tbsp/25 g/1 oz butter
8½ cups/1 kg/2 lb onions, sliced
¼ cup/1 oz/25 g flour
1 tsp mixed chopped herbs, preferably fresh
1 qt/1 L/1¾ pt vegetable stock (broth)
salt and freshly ground pepper
1 small French loaf (bread)
100 g/4 oz Mozzarella cheese, sliced
1 tbsp chopped parsley

PREPARATION

☛ Melt the butter in the browning dish, remove from the oven and stir in the onions. Return to the microwave and cook on high power for 6 minutes, stirring once.

☛ Sprinkle the flour over the onions and return for a further 1 minute on full power.

☛ Add the herbs, vegetable stock and seasoning, stir well and cook, covered, on full power for 10 minutes.

☛ Toast the French bread, cover it with slices of Mozzarella and melt under the grill (broiler) or in the microwave for a few seconds.

☛ Arrange the bread and cheese in the soup bowl, pour over the onion soup and sprinkle generously with chopped parsley.

Minestrone

INGREDIENTS

SERVES 4
½ cup/100 g/4 oz haricot (navy) beans, soaked for 12 hours
2 onions, finely chopped (minced)
2 carrots, chopped
1 small turnip, peeled and chopped
½ cauliflower, cut in florets
1 bouquet garni
1 bay leaf
1 vegetable stock cube
salt and pepper
1 leek, sliced
¼ small cabbage, shredded
1 tbsp parsley, chopped
½ cup/50 g/2 oz grated Parmesan cheese

PREPARATION

☛ Rinse the soaked beans under running cold water. Place in a large bowl or casserole with 1 qt/1 L/1¾ pt water. Cook on full power for 15 minutes.
☛ While the beans are cooking prepare the remaining vegetables. Add the onions, carrots and turnip to the beans and cook for 8 minutes on full power. Then add the cauliflower florets, stir in the bouquet garni, bay leaf, vegetable stock cube and season with salt and pepper. Cook for a further 10 minutes on full power.
☛ Finally add the leeks and cabbage and cook for a further 8 minutes on full power. Test to see if the vegetables are tender: if they need further cooking, switch to full power for a further 2–3 minutes.

TO SERVE

Sprinkle each bowl of soup with chopped parsley and serve the Parmesan cheese separately.

Leek and Potato Soup

INGREDIENTS

SERVES 4
2 potatoes, peeled and diced
1 qt/1 L/1¾ pt vegetable stock (broth)
2 tbsp/25 g/1 oz butter
1 onion, peeled and diced
2 leeks, washed and sliced
2 tsp chives, chopped
salt and pepper
1 bouquet garni
1 tbsp chopped parsley
wholemeal (wholewheat) bread

PREPARATION

☛ Place the potatoes in a large microwave dish and pour the vegetable stock (broth) over the potatoes. Cook on full power for 10 minutes.

☛ Melt the butter in a browning dish, add the onion and leeks and cook on full power for 5 minutes.

☛ Add the leeks and onion to the potato stock with the chives, seasoning and bouquet garni. Cook at full power for 10 minutes. Taste for seasoning, checking that the potatoes are cooked. If not, cook for a further 2 minutes on full power.

TO SERVE

Sprinkle with chopped parsley and serve with slices of wholemeal (wholewheat) bread.

VARIATION

Blend, liquidize or put through a vegetable mill or food processor.

☛ Add ¼ cup/50 ml/2 fl oz cream and serve hot or cold.

Tomato and Carrot Soup

INGREDIENTS

SERVES 4

2 cups/450 ml/¾ pt vegetable stock (broth)

¾ lb/350 g/12 oz carrots, thinly sliced

1 onion, thinly sliced

2 × 14 oz/400 g/14 oz cans plum tomatoes or
2 lb/1 kg/2 lb tomatoes, skinned

¼ tsp basil

salt and pepper

2 drops soy sauce

⅔ tbsp cream (optional)

PREPARATION

☛ Add the cold stock to the carrots and blanch for 5 minutes at full power.

☛ Add the onion to the carrots with all the other ingredients except the cream. Cook on full power for 10 minutes, reduce to half power and cook for a further 20 minutes. Test the carrots; if they are not soft enough cook for a further 5 minutes on full.

☛ Allow to cool slightly and then blend, sieve or purée in a food processor. Taste for seasoning.

TO SERVE

Reheat in individual bowls or in a large bowl as required, sprinkle a swirl of cream on top of each portion, if liked, and garnish with a few slivers of raw carrot.

Braised Brussels Sprouts with Nuts

INGREDIENTS

SERVES 4
2 lb/1 kg/2 lb Brussels sprouts, washed
1 lemon, rind grated, juice squeezed
salt and pepper
2½ cups/600 ml/1 pt Béchamel (White) Sauce (see page 19)
1 cup/100 g/4 oz peanuts, chopped
¼ tsp grated nutmeg
1 tbsp chopped parsley

PREPARATION

☛ Prepare the brussels sprouts by trimming the stalks and cutting a cross in the centre of each stalk. Place them in a large microwave dish with 1 cup/225 ml/8 fl oz water with the little lemon juice and salt. Cook on full power for 10 minutes, and leave to stand for 2 minutes. Test for doneness: if they are too crunchy, cook for a further 2 minutes.

☛ Drain the sprouts, reserving the water. Use half the cooking water made up with milk for the Béchamel Sauce (see page 19).

☛ Arrange the cooked sprouts in a serving dish with a little grated lemon rind sprinkled on top. Mix the nuts with the nutmeg and parsley.

☛ Coat the sprouts with the Béchamel (White) Sauce and top with the nut mixture. Reheat for 4 minutes at full power.

Poached Eggs with Red Wine Sauce

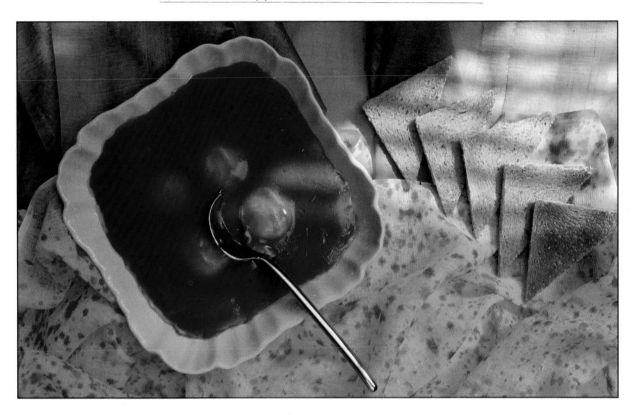

INGREDIENTS

SERVES 4

2 leeks, white parts only, thinly sliced

2 tbsp/25 g/1 oz butter

1 cup/225 ml/8 fl oz red wine

salt and freshly ground pepper

grated nutmeg

1 bouquet garni

¼ cup/25 g/1 oz flour

4 eggs

PREPARATION

☞ Put the leeks into a dish with 2–3 tbsp water and cook on full power for 2 minutes. Remove from the oven and drain.

☞ Melt half the butter in a dish in the microwave oven for 1 minute, add the leeks and stir well. Cook for 3 minutes on full power.

☞ Add the wine, seasoning and bouquet garni and cook at full power for 5 minutes. Remove the leeks

from the oven and discard the bouquet garni.

☞ Mix the flour with the remaining butter until the mixture is crumbly. Add the butter and flour to the leeks in small pieces and beat with a whisk until the mixture is smooth. Cook at full power for 5 minutes and then check the sauce is smooth and well seasoned.

☞ Grease a dish which will hold 4 eggs. Break the eggs into the dish, and prick the yolk with a sterilized skewer or large needle. Melt a little butter and pour onto the eggs, cover with kitchen towel and cook for 2 minutes. Allow to stand to finish cooking for about 30 seconds.

☞ Pour the sauce over the eggs and reheat and serve immediately.

TO SERVE

Serve with crisp toast. This makes an excellent starter but the wine must be of good quality.

Pizza

Making pizzas using the microwave oven to prove the dough is even faster than making a pie or a flan. However the pizza is better cooked in a conventional oven for a crisp crust. A special browning dish is available in the shape of a pizza which will give a crisp base if the dish is heated for 5 minutes, then brushed over with oil. This dish is also useful for re-heating frozen pizzas. If using dried yeast, follow the manufacturer's directions if they conflict with recipe directions below.

INGREDIENTS

SERVES 4

4 cups/450 g/1 lb strong plain (all purpose) flour
1 tsp salt
15 g/½ oz fresh (compressed) yeast or
1 envelope dried (dry active) yeast and ½ tsp sugar
1 tbsp oil
1¼ cups/300 ml/½ pt tepid water

PREPARATION

☛ Sift the flour into a bowl with the salt. If using fresh yeast, cream the yeast with a little of the water. If using dried yeast, mix the sugar with the water. Whisk, and leave for 10–15 minutes to froth.

☛ Add the yeast, oil and water to the flour and mix to a smooth elastic dough on a floured board. Knead for 5 minutes, or until the dough is smooth and elastic. Clean the bowl, return the dough to it and cover with cling film (plastic wrap). Turn on to full power for 15 seconds and then allow to stand for 10 minutes.

☛ Microwave the dough for a further 15 seconds and allow to stand for another 10 minutes. Repeat this 15 second burst once more leaving to stand as before.

☛ The dough should now have doubled in size and is ready to be made into pizzas.

Note: Dough can also be made with wholemeal (wholewheat) flour, or half wholemeal (wholewheat), half white flour.

Pizza Napolitana

INGREDIENTS

SERVES 4

4 rounds bread dough, about 20 cm (8 in) in diameter
¼ cup/50 ml/2 fl oz olive oil
1 garlic clove, peeled
2 × 14 oz/425 g/14 oz cans tomatoes
salt and pepper
2 tsp chopped basil
24 black olives
225 g/8 oz Mozzarella cheese, sliced

PREPARATION

☛ Preheat a conventional oven to 220°C/450°F/Gas Mark 8.

☛ Oil 2 baking (cookie) sheets or 4 flan rings. If you use flan rings you will have a deep dish pizza. For a thin pizza, roll out the dough thinly and shape into rounds on the baking (cookie) sheets. Brush the dough with olive oil.

☛ Rub the dough with a cut clove of garlic. If you like a stronger flavour, crush the remainder into the tomatoes.

☛ Mash the tomatoes with a wooden spoon and season well with salt and pepper. Add the chopped basil. Cover the rounds of dough with the tomato mixture. Arrange the black olives and Mozzarella cheese over the top.

☛ Brush the pizza with oil. Bake thin pizzas for 12 minutes and for thicker pizzas reduce the oven temperature to 180°C/350°F/Gas Mark 4 and bake for a further 10 minutes.

Note It is possible to cook a quick pizza in the microwave but it must be eaten quickly or the dough will become tough. Take a browning dish or pizza tray and heat for 4–5 minutes at full power. Brush with oil, lay the dough in the dish, cover it with the filling and cook on full for 5 minutes. Allow to stand for 3 minutes. The pizza is tasty but looks rather pale.

RIGHT: *Pizza Napolitana*

Celery Bake

INGREDIENTS

SERVES 4

1 tbsp vegetable oil
2 onions, chopped
1 head of celery, trimmed and sliced into 2½ cm/1 in pieces
1 cup/100 g/4 oz peanuts, coarsely chopped
1 green (bell) pepper, deseeded and sliced
1 can condensed celery soup
¼ cup/50 ml/2 fl oz milk
½ tsp soy sauce
¼ tsp ginger
1 tbsp sherry (optional)
6 pineapple rings
salt and freshly ground pepper
1 tbsp chopped parsley

PREPARATION

☛ Heat the oil in a browning dish for 1 minute. Add the onion and celery and cook on full power for 3 minutes. Remove from the oven and stir.

☛ Add the peanuts to the vegetables with the pepper and mix well.

☛ Pour the soup and all the other liquid ingredients into a bowl and whisk well until mixed. Chop two of the pineapple rings, add to the liquid and pour over the vegetables. Cook on full power for 10 minutes. Stand for 3 minutes, then cook on half power for another 15 minutes.

☛ Arrange the remaining slices of pineapple on top and cook for 1 minute.

TO SERVE

Sprinkle with chopped parsley.

VARIATION

This bake can also be made with 2½ cups/600 ml/ 1 pt Béchamel Sauce (see page 19) if this is preferred to canned soup.

Winter Chilli (Chili)

INGREDIENTS

SERVES 4

¼ cup/50 g/2 oz butter

2 onions, chopped

1 garlic clove, peeled and crushed

2 carrots, diced

2½ cups/600 ml/1 pt vegetable stock (broth)

6 tomatoes, peeled and chopped

2 red (bell) peppers, deseeded, sliced

1 chilli (chili) pepper, deseeded, sliced

¼–½ tsp chilli (chili) powder

1 aubergine (eggplant), sliced

1 cup/100 g/4 oz mushrooms, sliced

1 tbsp cornflour (cornstarch)

1 can kidney beans

1 tbsp tomato purée (paste)

2 tbsp sweet corn

chopped parsley

PREPARATION

☞ Melt the butter in the browning dish for 1 minute on full power.

☞ Add the onion and garlic and cook at full power for 1 minute. Add the carrots and vegetable stock (broth) and cook at full power for 5 minutes.

☞ Add the tomatoes, peppers, mushrooms, aubergine (eggplant) and chilli (chili) to the vegetable stock and cook on full power for 2 minutes.

☞ Blend the cornflour (cornstarch) with a little water and the tomato purée and add the chilli (chili) powder. Remove the casserole from the oven and stir in the tomato mixture until well blended. Return to the microwave and cook at full power for 5 minutes.

☞ Add the canned kidney beans and sweet corn and cook on full power for 10 minutes. Allow to stand for 5 minutes before serving.

TO SERVE

Sprinkle with parsley.

Striped Cabbage Casserole

INGREDIENTS

SERVES 4
2 tbsp/25 g/1 oz butter
1 onion, diced
1 parsnip, diced
2 carrots, diced
½ lb/225 g/8 oz green cabbage, shredded thinly
½ lb/225 g/8 oz red cabbage, shredded thinly
14 oz/400 g/14 oz can tomatoes or 2 lb/1 kg/2 lb fresh tomatoes, skinned
2½ cups/600 ml/1 pt vegetable stock (broth)
tomato purée (paste)
½ tsp soy sauce
salt and freshly ground pepper
1 tsp dried mixed herbs

PREPARATION

☛ Heat the butter in a browning dish for 1 minute on full power.

☛ Add the onion, parsnip and carrots to the butter and cook on full power for 1 minute. Stir and cook for another 2 minutes.

☛ Reserve about one quarter of each colour of cabbage on a plate for the top of the casserole, and add the rest to the tomatoes. Add the stock (broth) purée (paste), soy sauce, seasoning and herbs and mix well. Pour this over the vegetables and stir to distribute evenly.

☛ Cook on full power for 10 minutes. Remove and stir, tasting for seasoning. Arrange the remaining cabbage in alternate red and green stripes on top of the casserole. Return to the microwave oven and cook for a further 5 minutes on full power. The cabbage should be fairly crisp.

Welsh Rarebit

INGREDIENTS

SERVES 2
1 cup/100 g/4 oz Cheddar cheese, grated (shredded)
2 oz/50 g/2 oz blue cheese
2 tsp French mustard
pinch of salt
freshly ground black pepper
2 tbsp milk or 2 tbsp whisky or beer
4 slices of toast

PREPARATION

☛ Place all the ingredients except the toast in a medium-sized deep bowl and mix well.
☛ Cook for 2 minutes on full power. Stir well and remove after another 2–3 minutes or when bubbling. Pour over the pieces of toast and brown under a hot grill (broiler)

TO SERVE

Eat as a snack or serve with a vegetable casserole. Use milk if serving with vegetables.

Home-Baked Beans

This has long been a great favourite of mine but it takes so long – about 6 hours – to cook in the oven. The microwave oven solves this problem and although still not quick to make, it requires very little attention.

INGREDIENTS

SERVES 4
2¼ cups/450 g/1 lb haricot (navy) beans
2 tbsp vegetable oil
2 onions, diced
1 aubergine (eggplant), diced
2 × 14 oz/400 g/14 oz can of tomatoes or 2 lb/1 kg/2 lb tomatoes, skinned
2 garlic cloves, peeled
¼ cup/3 tbsp tomato purée (paste)
2 tbsp vinegar
1 tsp soy sauce
2½ cups/600 ml/1 pt vegetable stock (broth)
2 tbsp molasses
salt and freshly ground pepper
1 tsp mustard
½ tsp thyme
1 tbsp chopped parsley

PREPARATION

☛ Soak the beans overnight in cold water to cover. Drain. Put the beans in a saucepan of cold water to cover and bring to the boil on the stove top for 10 minutes.

☛ Heat the oil in the microwave oven in a browning dish for 2 minutes. Add the onions and cook on full power for a further 2 minutes.

☛ Put half the onions in a suitable microwave casserole and cover with a layer of beans.

☛ Mix the aubergine (eggplant) and chopped tomatoes with all the remaining ingredients.

☛ Arrange half the mixture onto the beans and onions, add the remaining beans and cover with the other half of the mixture.

☛ Place the casserole in the microwave oven and cook at full power for 15 minutes. Allow to rest for 5 minutes.

☛ Cook on half power for a further 30 minutes, test the beans, and stir the mixture. If the beans are still firm, cook on full power for a further 10 minutes.

TO SERVE

These beans can be served on toast as a snack or cold with salad or as part of a starter.

Sweet and Sour Cabbage

This is one of the blessings of the microwave as the conventional cooking time for the same dish is 2 hours.

INGREDIENTS

SERVES 4

¼ cup/50 g/2 oz butter

1 onion, peeled and diced

1½ lb/750 g/1½ lb red cabbage, thinly sliced

2 cooking (tart) apples, peeled and diced

salt and freshly ground pepper

1 tsp soy sauce

¼ cup/50 ml/2 fl oz wine vinegar

1 tbsp sugar

3 tbsp/2 tbsp redcurrant jelly

PREPARATION

☛ Melt the butter in a large dish. Add the onions and cook on full power for 1 minute.

☛ Arrange the onion, cabbage and apples in layers, seasoning each one with salt and pepper and a sprinkling of soy sauce.

☛ Measure the vinegar in a jug with the same amount of water. Pour it over the cabbage and cook, covered, on full for 10 minutes. Allow to stand for 3 minutes.

☛ Add the sugar and the redcurrant jelly, mix well and cook for a further 10 minutes on full power. If the texture is too crunchy, cook for a further 5 minutes.

TO SERVE

Allow to cool if possible as this dish is even better if kept for 1–2 days. Reheat in the microwave on full power, stir and cook for a further 3 minutes. It is also excellent served as a cold salad.

Pork Marrakesh

Weight Watchers Recipe

by *Momentum Cookbook*, from Weight Watchers Publishing Group

★ ★ ★ ★ ⯪

Course: main meals
***PointsPlus*® Value:** 6
Servings: 4
Preparation Time: 6 min
Cooking Time: 240 min
Level of Difficulty: Easy

Serve with couscous because its ideal for soaking up all the great sauce.

Ingredients

2 tsp olive oil
piece 1 pound(s) lean boneless pork chop(s), 4 (1⁄4-pound) trimmed
3/4 tsp table salt
1/4 tsp black pepper
3 small uncooked red onion(s), thinly sliced
12 halves dried apricot halves, sliced
1 cup 3/4 cup(s) canned unsweetened pineapple juice
2 tsp ginger root, fresh, peeled and minced
1/2 tsp dried thyme
1 average cinnamon stick(s)
1/4 cup(s) cilantro, fresh, chopped

Instructions

Heat 1 teaspoon of the oil in a large nonstick skillet over medium-high heat. Sprinkle the pork chops with 1⁄4 teaspoon of the salt and the pepper. Add the chops to the skillet and cook until browned, about 2 minutes on each side Transfer to a plate.

Reduce the heat to medium and add the onions, the remaining 1 teaspoon oil, and the remaining 1⁄2 teaspoon salt to the skillet. Cook, stirring, until the onions are golden, about 10 minutes.

Place half of the apricots and half of the onions in the bottom of a 5- or 6-quart slow cooker. Top with the pork chops and the remaining onions and apricots. Add the *pine*apple juice, ginger, thyme, and cinnamon stick. Cover and cook until the pork is fork-tender, 3 – 4 hours on high or 6 – 8 hours on low. Remove the cinnamon stick and serve sprinkled with the cilantro. Yields 1 pork chop and 1⁄2 cup onion mixture per serving.

3 cups extra water because of slow cooker size

Tart Apple Pork

Weight Watchers Recipe

by *Winner's Circle*, from Weight Watchers Publishing Group

★ ★ ★ ★ ⯪

Course: light meals
***PointsPlus*®** Value: 7
Servings: 4
Preparation Time: 10 min
Cooking Time: 30 min
Level of Difficulty: Easy

Apples and fresh herbs complement the pork, giving it the moisture and flavor her husband wants.

Ingredients

16 oz lean boneless pork chop(s), center-cut, trimmed of all visible fat
1 Tbsp rosemary, fresh, chopped
1 Tbsp thyme, fresh, fresh, chopped
1/2 tsp table salt
1/4 tsp black pepper, freshly ground
2 tsp canola oil
2 medium fresh apple(s), Granny Smith, peeled, cored, and sliced
1 large uncooked onion(s), thinly sliced
2/3 cup(s) apple juice, unsweetened variety
2 Tbsp honey mustard

Instructions

Sprinkle the chops with the rosemary, thyme, salt, and pepper. Heat 1 teaspoon of the oil in a large nonstick skillet over medium-high heat. Add the chops and cook until browned and cooked through, 4–5 minutes on each side; transfer to a plate and cover to keep warm.

Heat the remaining 1 teaspoon oil in the same skillet over medium heat. Add the apples and onion. Cook, stirring occasionally, until tender and golden, about 8 minutes. Stir in the apple juice and honey mustard; bring to a boil. Reduce the heat and simmer, uncovered, until the sauce thickens slightly, about 5 minutes. Return chops to pan and cook, turning once, to heat through, about 2 minutes. Yields 1 chop with 1/2 cup apple mixture per serving.

Layered Leeks

INGREDIENTS

SERVES 4   9 6
            6

2–3 potatoes, peeled and thinly sliced

2 parsnips, thinly sliced

1 large onion, thinly sliced

¼ cup/50 g/2 oz butter

salt and pepper

1¼ cups/300 ml/½ pt milk

3 leeks, washed and sliced

¼ cup/50 ml/2 fl oz cream

¼ tsp nutmeg

2 tbsp grated cheese *Cheddar*

PREPARATION

350° oven

☞ Cut the potato, parsnip and onion into similar sized chunks.

☞ Butter the 1 qt/1 L/2½ pt dish and arrange half of the potato and all of the parsnips and onion in layers. Season each layer well and pour the milk over the top.

☞ Microwave for 5 minutes at full power and then leave to stand for 2 minutes. Cook at full power for a further 5 minutes. *10 min.*

☞ Arrange the leeks on top of the other vegetables, season with nutmeg and top with the remaining potatoes. Pour the cream over the vegetables and dot them with butter. *30 min*

☞ Cook in the oven for 10 minutes on full power. Check to see if the vegetables are done: you may need a further 5–7 minutes at full power, depending on thickness of vegetables and type of potatoes used. *10 min*

TO SERVE

Sprinkle with cheese and brown under the grill (broiler) for a golden finish.

Lentil Loaf

INGREDIENTS

SERVES 4

1¼ cups/225 g/8 oz lentils

¼ cup/50 ml/2 fl oz oil

1 onion, diced

½ lb/225 ml/8 oz mushrooms, sliced

2 tbsp/25 g/1 oz butter

1¼ cups/300 ml/½ pt vegetable stock (broth)

¼ tsp paprika

salt and pepper

1 tsp fresh herbs, chopped

1 egg, beaten

½ cup/50 ml/2 fl oz cream

1 tbsp chopped parsley or 2 tomatoes, skinned and sliced

PREPARATION

☛ Wash the lentils under cold running water and remove any discoloured seeds. Pour 1¼ cups/300 ml/½ pt boiling water over the lentils and allow to stand for 5 minutes before draining.

☛ Heat the oil in a casserole on high for 1 minute, add the onion and cook on full power for 3 minutes.

☛ Remove the onion from the oil with a slotted spoon and reserve. Cook the mushrooms in the oil and the butter for 3 minutes, covered. Allow to stand for 2 minutes.

☛ In a separate bowl, cook the lentils in the vegetable stock for 7 minutes on full power. Leave to stand for 3 minutes or until most of the liquid is absorbed.

☛ Mix the cooked lentils with the onion, seasonings, herbs, egg and cream.

☛ Spread half the mixture in a microwave loaf pan or a 3 cups/700 ml/1½ pt ovenproof glass bowl. Arrange the mushrooms over the mixture and add the remaining lentil mixture. Smooth the surface with a spoon, cover and cook for 5 minutes on full power. Allow to stand for 4 minutes before turning out on to a heated serving dish.

TO SERVE

Sprinkle with chopped parsley or sliced tomatoes. Serve with Tomato Sauce (see page 15) or 1¼ cups Béchamel Sauce (see page 19) with 1½ cups/100 g/ 4 oz mushrooms, chopped finely.

VARIATION

Cheese and Lentil Loaf. Add ½ cup/50 g/2 oz grated cheese to the lentil mixture before cooking.

Candied Sweet Potatoes with Orange

INGREDIENTS

SERVES 4

2 medium-sized sweet potatoes

⅔ cup/150 ml/¼ pt orange juice

¼ cup/50 g/2 oz soft brown sugar

2 tbsp/25 g/1 oz butter

1 tsp nutmeg

½ tsp cinnamon

1 orange

PREPARATION

☛ Peel and slice the sweet potatoes into 12 mm/½ in slices and place in a casserole. Pour the orange juice over them and cook, on full power, for 10 minutes.

☛ Remove the sweet potatoes from the dish to a suitable serving dish and reserve.

☛ Mix the sugar, butter, nutmeg and cinnamon with the orange juice and stir well. Microwave for 5 minutes at full power until syrupy.

☛ Pour the syrup over the sweet potatoes and microwave at full power for another 4 minutes.

☛ Cut the peel from the orange, remove all the white pith, and cut into 8 slices.

☛ Decorate each end of the dish with the peel slices and return to the oven for 1½ minutes.

Winter Vegetable Casserole

INGREDIENTS

SERVES 4

2 tbsp/25 g/1 oz butter

1 onion, diced

1 potato, sliced

2 carrots, diced

1 parsnip, diced

1 leek, sliced

1 red (bell) pepper, deseeded and sliced

½ tsp thyme

½ tsp marjoram

1 tbsp tomato purée (paste)

1 cup/225 ml/8 fl oz vegetable stock (broth)

salt and pepper

1 tsp soy sauce

½ cup/50 g/2 oz cheese, grated

1 tbsp parsley, chopped

wholemeal (wholewheat) bread

PREPARATION

☛ Melt the butter in large browning dish, add the onion and cook for 2 minutes at full power. Remove.

☛ Prepare the potatoes, carrots, parsnips and leeks and cover with boiling water in a bowl. Blanch in the microwave for 5 minutes at high. Drain and use the water to make up the stock if using a cube.

☛ Add the blanched vegetables, sweet pepper and remaining butter to the onion in the browning dish. Cook for 3 minutes on full power.

☛ Add the thyme, marjoram, tomato purée (paste) and stock (broth). Season well with salt and pepper, stir and cook at high for 15 minutes.

☛ Check the vegetables at this stage to see if they are done: they will still be crunchy. Cook for a further 2 minutes if preferred softer.

☛ Serve hot sprinkled with cheese, parsley and slices of wholemeal (wholewheat) bread.

Nut and Vegetable Cobbler

INGREDIENTS

great fun *loved*

oven 350°

SERVES 4	
1 lb/450 g/1 lb canned butter (lima) beans	8
3 ½ lb/225 g/8 oz potatoes, peeled and cubed	6
1 small green chilli (chili) pepper, deseeded and sliced	
½ lb/225 g/8 oz carrots, sliced	O
2 celery stalks, sliced	O
1 onion, sliced	O
1 small can tomatoes *15oz*	O
2 dessert apples, cored and chopped	O
1 vegetable stock cube	O
salt and pepper	O *45 min*
TOPPING:	
1 cup/100 g/4 oz plain (all purpose) flour	10
1 tsp baking powder	O
salt and pepper	O
Plain Dry Ground 1 tsp French mustard	O
Italian ½ tsp dried mixed herbs ~ *1 Tb*	O
¼ cup/50 g/2 oz butter	9
mozzarella ¼ cup/25 g/1 oz grated cheese	1
½ cup/50 g/2 oz finely ground hazelnuts (filberts)	5
¼ cup/3 tbsp cold water	O *15-20 min*

4/39/10   till browned
6/39/7½   rolls or topping

PREPARATION

☛ Drain the butter (lima) beans, reserving their liquid, and combine with all the vegetables and the apples in a large casserole.

☛ Heat the juice from the butter (lima) beans for 2 minutes on full power, then dissolve the stock cube in it.

☛ Pour the stock over the vegetables and season well. Cover with pierced cling film (plastic wrap), or a plate, and cook on full power for 12 minutes, stirring after 4 and 8 minutes.

☛ Sift the flour, salt and pepper and mustard into a bowl. Add the herbs.

☛ Rub in the butter until the mixture resembles fine breadcrumbs. Stir in the cheese and nuts. Add the water and mix to a soft, elastic dough. Shape into 8 balls and place them around the outside of the vegetables. Cover with the lid or pierced cling film (plastic wrap) and microwave on full power for 7 minutes.

Potato and Mushroom Pie

INGREDIENTS

SERVES 4

1 lb/450 g/1 lb potatoes, peeled and sliced

2½ cups/225 g/8 oz mushrooms

1 onion

salt

freshly ground pepper

grated nutmeg

⅔ cup/150 ml/¼ pt milk

3 tbsp/2 tbsp cream

4 eggs

¼ cup/1 oz/25 g grated cheese

1 tbsp chopped parsley

PREPARATION

☞ Arrange a layer of potatoes on a buttered dish of approximately 1 qt/1 L/1¾ pt capacity.

☞ Slice the mushrooms, with trimmed stalks still attached, and the onion. Layer the mushrooms and onion with the potatoes, seasoning betwen layers until all the ingredients are used. Make four hollows to hold the eggs. Add the milk and cream and cook on full power for 10 minutes.

☞ Stand for 6 minutes then microwave for 6 minutes on full power. Stand for another 5 minutes and then test the potatoes. If they are too hard, cook for a further 4 minutes on full power.

☞ Poach the four eggs in the microwave (see page 25).

☞ With a slotted spoon, lift the eggs carefully into the spaces on the vegetable casserole. Return to the microwave oven for 30 seconds to reheat.

TO SERVE

Sprinkle with grated cheese and if liked, brown under a very hot grill (broiler) for a few seconds. Serve sprinkled with chopped parsley and crisp triangles of brown toast.

Dal

INGREDIENTS

SERVES 4
1¼ cups/225 g/8 oz red lentils, washed
¼ cup/50 ml/2 fl oz vegetable oil
2 medium-sized onions, finely chopped
1 garlic clove, crushed
1 small fresh chilli (chili) pepper, deseeded and chopped
2½ cups/600 ml/1 pt vegetable stock
½ tsp turmeric
½ tsp garam masala or curry powder
salt and pepper
1 tomato, skinned
1 tbsp chopped fresh coriander (cilantro) or parsley

PREPARATION

☞ Wash the lentils carefully, removing any discoloured seeds. Pour boiling water over them and leave to soak for 15 minutes. Drain them.

☞ Heat the vegetable oil in a browning dish for 1 minute on full power. Add the onions finely to the oil with the garlic. Cook on full power for 2 minutes. Add the chilli (chili) pepper and cook for a further 2 minutes.

☞ Stir in the lentils, vegetable stock and the turmeric and garam masala or curry powder. Season with salt and pepper and mix well.

☞ Cook on full power for 10 minutes. Allow to stand for another 5 minutes and then cook for a further 10 minutes. The lentils should be tender.

TO SERVE

Arrange the sliced tomato on top and sprinkle with chopped coriander or parsley.

STANDING TIME

This is a most important stage of microwave cooking In the same way that a roast of meat or chicken is left to stand before carving, all food cooked in the microwave oven requires a short time to stand to complete the cooking process. This allows the heat created in the outer layers of the food by the microwaves to be conducted through to the inside.

A good example is a microwaved cake, which will look slightly soggy in the middle at the end of the cooking time, but will finish cooking and become firm during the standing time. It is easy to recognize this in a cake, less noticeable in a savoury dish, but the principle is the same. It is always better to undercook slightly if you are unsure of the timing. The wider the variety of dishes you cook in the microwave oven the more experienced you will become in judging the standing times. A thin layer of food will conduct heat more quickly than a solid mass and will therefore need less standing time.

PREPARING VEGETABLES FOR THE FREEZER

The microwave oven is useful for blanching small quantities of vegetables for the freezer. Do not prepare more than 1 lb/450 g at a time. If freezing large quantities of garden produce, it is better to blanch in the conventional way. To blanch 450 g/1 lb vegetables arrange in a large casserole, add ½ cup/125 ml/4 fl oz boiling water. Cover and microwave for half the cooking time; stir, cover again, and finish cooking. Plunge into ice cold water, drain and pack as usual.

Another convenient method is to pack the vegetables in heavy-gauge plastic bags and microwave them in the bags. Rinse the vegetables, pack them in the unsealed bags and microwave them for half the cooking time on one side. Turn the bag over and cook for the remaining blanching time. Expel the air and seal the bags before plunging them into ice cold water. Pat dry and store in the freezer. To cook the vegetables in the microwave oven, first remove the metal seal, if used, and cook in the bag.

PULSES AND BEANS

Dried pulses and beans are another very important part of a vegetarian diet and all these can be cooked with the minimum attention in the microwave oven. This includes dried peas (pea-beans), split peas, lentils, haricot (navy), kidney, lima, aduki and butter beans, black-eyed beans (peas), chick-peas (garbanzo) and all other dried beans. Pulses and beans require a long soaking time before cooking; the cooking times are similar to those for conventional cookery. Lentils are the only exception to the soaking rule. Overnight soaking is usually convenient but time can be saved by pouring boiling water over pulses and beans; they can then be cooked after 2–3 hours.

Chickpeas need soaking for 48 hours, or 12 hours if the boiling water method is used. These can take from 2–6 hours to cook by boiling, unless pressure cooked. However chickpeas will cook in the microwave in approximately 45–60 minutes.

To cook pulses and beans Drain the soaked beans. Wash lentils well and remove any discoloured seeds. Cover with fresh cold water, and start timing the cooking when the water has come to the boil. Add salt while there is still some liquid in the dish, about 10 minutes before the end of the cooking time, but never add salt at the beginning as this will harden the beans. Allow a standing time of 10–15 minutes.

RICE AND PASTA

Both these foods combine well with vegetables, vegetable sauces and vegetable casseroles, making rice and pasta an essential part of a vegetarian diet. White rice contains about 2.2 g, and pasta 4.2 g protein per 100 g/4 oz after cooking.

Because both foods absorb water during cooking, little time is saved by cooking them in the microwave oven. However, there is still the advantage of having the kitchen free from steam, and little or no attention is required during cooking. A large container is essential to allow the water to boil and for the expansion of the food as the water is absorbed.

RICE

Rice cooks perfectly every time in the microwave oven, whatever the type, and when all the water or stock is absorbed each rice grain is light fluffy and separate.

To make a savoury rice mixture, cook a finely diced onion and a deseeded, chopped pepper in 2 tablespoons oil for 2 minutes. Stir in the rice and finally add the boiling water. Use hot or cold as required.

To cook, pour the boiling, salted water on to the rice in the container and stir to allow the water to surround the rice. Time the rice after the water has returned to the boil. I find it best to rinse all types of rice before cooking in the microwave oven. To measure the amount of water needed, simply measure the rice in a cup and use 2 measures of boiling water to one of rice. ¾ cup/225 g/8 oz raw rice will yield 4–6 portions.

PASTA

It is only practicable to cook small quantities of pasta in the microwave oven. 1 to 2 portions is an ideal amount. Do not cook more than 100 g/4 oz–225 g/8 oz at one time. Pasta really needs the agitation of the fast boiling water to move it around during cooking and the results are more satisfactory when cooked by conventional boiling. To microwave pasta, first choose a suitable dish. For instance, a deep, rectangular dish is suitable for spaghetti; it is better to break long noodles into manageable strands. Place boiling water in the container with salt and a little oil and drop the pasta into the water. This stops the pasta sticking together, as it tends to do when boiling water is poured over the pasta. Stir, and start the timing when the water returns to the boil. Half-way through the cooking time, stir the pasta, and cover the dish with a lid or cling film (plastic wrap); finish the cooking.

TO COOK LASAGNE WITH SAUCES

Prepare the dish according to the recipe, but make sure that the sauces are not too thick as they will thicken during standing time. Allow the dish to stand for 20–30 minutes before cooking as this gives the lasagne time to absorb some of the moisture from the sauces and gives a better result. The same applies to home-made lasagne.

TO REHEAT PASTA AND RICE

Add a knob of butter and cover with cling film (plastic wrap). Allow 4 minutes on full power for 1 cup/225 g/8 oz cooked pasta or rice and 2 minutes standing time. The time will depend on the shape of the container, used but it is essential not too overcook it.

PREPARING AND COOKING VEGETABLES IN THE MICROWAVE

Vegetable	Preparation	Microwave blanching for freezing	Cook with water unless otherwise stated	Cooking Time Full Power (650W oven)	Standing Time	Serving suggestions
Globe Artichoke	Wash well and steep in water with vinegar for at least 10 mins. Trim stalks (see page 26 for further treatment)	Not advisable	1 tbsp/15 ml water + ½ tsp/5 ml lemon juice. Can be covered in cling film (plastic wrap)	5–7 mins, depending on size 10–12 mins	4 mins 4 mins	Hot: Hollandaise sauce lemon butter Cold: vinaigrette, mousseline sauce
Jerusalem Artichoke 1 lb/450 g	Peel and place at once in water with lemon juice to prevent discolouration	Best frozen as soup	½ cup/125 ml/ 4 fl oz + 1 tsp lemon juice	12–15 mins	5 mins	Hollandaise, Béchamel or cheese sauce
Aubergine (Eggplant) ½ lb/225 g/8 oz 4 halves	Wash, cut into slices or halves. Sprinkle with salt and allow to stand 20–30 mins to allow bitter juices to drain	Cook in a preheated browning dish in 3 tbsp oil for 4 mins. Otherwise freezes well in casseroles	½ cup/125 ml/ 4 fl oz ½ cup/125 ml/ 4 fl oz	7–8 mins 5 mins	4 mins 3 mins	Cheese or tomato sauce. Rice or pasta stuffings (see recipes for timings)
Asparagus 1 lb/450 g	Cut off woody part of stalk. Peel the remaining white stalk thinly	Blanch for 2–4 mins (see page 45 for amount of water and instructions)	¼ cup/50 ml/2 fl oz	8–10 mins depending on thickness	5 mins	Hot: melted butter, Hollandaise or cheese sauce Cold: vinaigrette or mousseline sauce
Broad Beans ½ lb/225 g/8 oz	Remove from the pod unless young enough to eat whole	Blanch in the microwave for 2 mins	¼ cup/50 ml/2 fl oz water	7 mins	3 mins	Hot: herbed butter, Béchamel sauce Cold: vinaigrette, mayonnaise
Runner (Italian) Beans 1 lb/450 g	Top, tail, string and slice	Blanch ½ lb/250 g/8 oz in the microwave for 2 mins	¼ cup/50 ml/2 fl oz salted water	10–12 mins	—	Hot: herbed butter, ½ tsp/2½ ml soy sauce mixed with 1 tsp/5 ml sherry
French (green) Beans ½ lb/225 g/8 oz	Top and tail, leave whole	Blanch for 2½ mins	¼ cup/50 ml/2 fl oz	5–6 mins	2 mins	Hot: sage butter Cold: vinaigrette sauce
Broccoli 1 lb/450 g	Remove outer leaves and trim stalks	Blanch for 2–3 mins	½ cup/125 ml/4 fl oz	8–10 mins	2 mins	Béchamel, cheese or Hollandaise sauce
Beetroot (Beets) 1 lb/450 g (sliced) ½ lb/225 g/8 oz (whole)	Peel and slice or prick whole beetroot and parcel in cling film (plastic wrap)	Not advisable except as soup	¼ cup/50 ml/2 fl oz for sliced Whole in cling wrap	8–9 mins 12–15 mins	2 mins 3 mins	Cold: vinaigrette Hot: Béchamel sauce or cream and cottage cheese
Brussels Sprouts 1 lb/450 g	Trim stalks, remove outer damaged leaves	Blanch for 2–3 mins depending on size	¼ cup/50 ml/ 2 fl oz	10–12 mins	3 mins	Hollandaise, cheese or Béchamel sauce
Cabbage 1 lb/450 g	Remove coarse, damaged outer leaves and shred just before cooking	Blanch for 2 mins	¼ cup/50 ml/ 2 fl oz	8 mins	2 mins	Herbed butter or Béchamel sauce
Cauliflower	Remove outer leaves, break into florets (flowerets) or leave whole	Blanch florets (flowerets) for 2½ mins	½ cup/125 ml/4 fl oz Whole cauliflower as above	10 mins 10–12 mins	2–3 mins 3 mins	Béchamel, cheese sauce or butter and garnish with sieved cooked egg white and yolk
Celery ½ lb/225 g/8 oz	Wash well and remove the strings, trim	Blanch sliced celery for 3 mins	¼ cup/50 ml/2 fl oz	10–12 mins	2 mins	Mix 1 egg yolk with 2–3 tbsp/30–45 ml thick cream Return to the microwave for 1 min
Celeriac	Remove root and cut into pieces to prepare. Drop into water with vinegar added to prevent discolouration	As for celery	As for celery	As for celery	As for celery	
Corn on the Cob 2	Either wash and trim, removing husk or cook in the husk	Blanch without husks for 3 mins	½ cup/125 ml/4 fl oz	8 mins	2 mins	Herbed butter
Courgettes (Zucchini) 1 lb/450 g	Trim the ends, slice and sprinkle with salt, allow to stand for 30 mins. Drain on kitchen paper	Blanch sliced courgettes for 2 mins	2 tsp or 2 tbsp/ 25 g/1 oz butter	6–8 mins	2 mins	Use in mixed vegetable casseroles. Lemon butter
Leeks 1 lb/450 g	Remove coarse green tops, roots and any outside damaged leaves. Make a cross cut in the leafy part and wash well under cold running water	Slice and blanch for 2 mins Whole 3½ mins	¼ cup/50 ml/2 fl oz or cook in 2 tbsp/ 25 g/1 oz butter	8 mins	5 mins	Béchamel or cheese sauce

PREPARING AND COOKING VEGETABLES IN THE MICROWAVE

Vegetable Marrow (Squash)	Halve, peel and remove pith (white part) and seeds. Cut into 1 in/2 cm slices	Better frozen, mashed as purée or blanched for 4 mins and stuffed whole	¼ cup/50 ml/2 fl oz	8–10 mins	5 mins	Béchamel, cheese or tomato sauce
Mushrooms ½ lb/225 g/8 oz	Peel if wild, wash cultivated variety	Cook in 2 tbsp/ 1 oz/25 g butter for 2 mins	¼ cup/50 ml/2 fl oz vegetable stock or in butter	5 mins	2 mins	Chopped herbs. Béchamel or cheese sauce
Okra 1 lb/450 g	Wash, top and tail. Sprinkle with salt and 1 tsp lemon juice. Allow to stand for 20–30 mins. Rinse	Best frozen in vegetable casseroles	¼ cup/50 ml/2 fl oz or same of oil	8–9 mins	2 mins	Curry, tomato or yogurt sauce
Onions ½ lb/225 g/8 oz Whole	Peel, slice or dice. Small whole onions should be peeled	Blanch for 2 mins or cook in butter. Blanch for 4 mins	¼ cup/50 ml/2 fl oz water or oil	6 mins 8–10 mins	2 mins 10 mins	Parsley, Béchamel, cheese or tomato sauce
Parsnips	Top and tail, peel thinly	Blanch for 3–4 mins. Only freeze young tender parsnips unless in soup or casseroles	½ cup/125 ml/4 fl oz	10 mins	5–10 mins	Parsley, Béchamel or cheese sauce
Peas 1½ cups/225 g/8 oz after shelling	Remove from pods	Blanch 1–2 mins	¼ cup/50 ml/2 fl oz water and a sprig of mint	10 mins	5 mins	2 tbsp/25 g/1 oz butter
Peppers, Bell or Chilli (Chili) ½ lb/225 g/8 oz	Deseed and wash. Slice or halve	Blanch for 2 mins	¼ cup/50 ml/ 2 fl oz water or oil	5 mins	2 mins	Cold: vinaigrette Hot: pasta or rice stuffings
Potatoes, old 2 × ½ lb/225 g/8 oz	Wash and scrub skins. Prick the skins and wrap in kitchen towels	Not advisable except cooked as a topping for savoury dishes or in a casserole		12 mins	5 mins wrapped in foil	Herb butters, cottage cheese and chives
Potatoes, new 1 lb/450 g/1 lb	Wash thoroughly and leave whole	Not advisable	½ cup/125 ml/4 fl oz	12 mins	5 mins	Herb butter or butter and 2 tbsp/ 25 g coarse oatmeal
Spinach 1 lb/450 g	Remove thick stalks and wash well	Blanch for 1½ mins	2 tsp/10 ml	6–8 mins	5 mins	Herb butter or cheese sauce
Tomatoes 4	Wash and halve	Freeze as purée	Arrange halves in a round dish around the circumference. Brush with melted butter	5 mins	5 mins	Tarragon butter or savoury stuffings
Turnips, Swedes (Rutabaga) 1 lb/450 g	Top and tail, peel thinly if young but more thickly if old	Freeze only if young and tender unless in casseroles Blanch 4 mins	½ cup/125 ml/4 fl oz	12 mins	10 mins	Rosemary butter

COOKING PASTA AND RICE IN THE MICROWAVE

	To cook	Cooking Time	Standing Time	To serve
Thin pasta – Tagliatelle noodles Dried ½ lb/225 g/8 oz Fresh ½ lb/225 g/8 oz	Sprinkle into 1 qt/1 l/1¾ pt boiling salted water with 2 tsp oil added	On full power 5–6 mins 3–5 mins	3–4 mins 2 mins	Drain and toss in a little melted butter with a pinch (dash) of grated nutmeg and freshly ground pepper
Spaghetti ½ lb/225 g/8 oz	Put into a large dish with 1 qt/1 l/1¾ pt boiling salted water. Stir half way through cooking time and cover with cling wrap for remaining cooking time	12 mins	2 mins	As above, then mix sauce with pasta and reheat for 1–2 mins
Macaroni ½ lb/225 g/8 oz	Sprinkle into 1 qt/1 L/1¾ pt of boiling water with 2 tsp oil added. Stir half way through cooking time	15 mins	2 mins	Drain as above. Mix with cheese or mushroom sauce
Pasta shells ½ lb/225 g/8 oz	Sprinkle into 1½ qt/1½ pt boiling salted water. Stir twice during cooking time	16 mins	2 mins	As above, mix with tomato, Béchamel or mushroom sauce etc. Use cold in salads
Long grain rice ½ lb/225 g/8 oz 1 cup/100 g/4 oz	Rinse under cold water. For each cup or measure of rice add 2 of boiling salted water. Or add to 2 cups/16 fl oz/¾ pt boiling salted water	12 mins 10 mins	3 mins 3 mins	Use to accompany curries and savoury vegetable dishes. Use cold in salads
Prefluffed or Easy-cook (minute) rice	As above	12 mins	5 mins	
Easy-cook brown rice	As above	12 mins	5 mins	
Brown rice	As above	25 mins	5 mins